REGNUM STUDIES IN MISSION

Searching for Heaven in the Real World

A Sociological Discussion of Conversion in the Arab World

Series Preface

Regnum Studies in Mission are born from the lived experience of Christians and Christian communities in mission, especially but not solely in the fast growing churches among the poor of the world. These churches have more to tell than stories of growth. They are making significant impacts on their cultures in the cause of Christ. They are producing 'cultural products' which express the reality of Christian faith, hope and love in their societies.

Regnum Studies in Mission are the fruit often of rigorous research to the highest international standards and always of authentic Christian engagement in the transformation of people and societies. And these are for the world. The formation of Christian theology, missiology and practice in the twenty-first century will depend to a great extent on the active participation of growing churches contributing biblical and culturally appropriate expressions of Christian practice to inform World Christianity.

Series Editors

A full listing of titles in this series
appears at the end of this book

REGNUM STUDIES IN MISSION

Searching for Heaven in the Real World

A Sociological Discussion of Conversion in the Arab World

Kathryn Ann Kraft

First published 2012 by Regnum Books International

Regnum is an imprint of the Oxford Centre for Mission Studies
St. Philip and St. James Church
Woodstock Road
Oxford, OX2 6HR, UK
www.ocms.ac.uk/regnum

09 08 07 06 05 04 03 8 7 6 5 4 3 2 1

British Library Cataloguing in Publication Data
A catalogue record for this book is available from the British Library

ISBN: 978-1-506477-32-9

Typeset by Words by Design
Cover design by Words by Design

The financial assistance of Robin and Nancy Wainwright of the Catlin Foundation towards this publication is gratefully acknowledged.

Distributed by 1517 Media in the US and Canada

Dedication

As I was nearing the end of this research project, I was given a beautiful painting of an Egyptian Nubian woman peering out of a rustic wooden door. The woman is beautiful, her head loosely covered in a traditional scarf and her hand decorated with henna. Is this a sign of her marriage, or is she just a young woman with a zest for life? What intrigued me so much about this painting, though, was the look in her eyes: an inspiring combination of curiosity, boldness and innocence. Those eyes conveyed to me the spirit of Muslim Arab women who had chosen a different faith, many of whom have remained too deeply sheltered by their home communities for me to ever actually look them in the eyes.

This book is dedicated to my Arab sisters, especially those who, like the Nubian woman, are peering out.

Contents

Dedication v
Acknowledgements ix

Chapter 1
Introduction 1
Background to the Topic 2
A Word on Terminology, Sociology and Conversion 4
Background: Why do People Convert? 6
Context 10
Summary of Methodology 13
Organisation of Chapters 16

Chapter 2
The Perfect Researcher 19
Insiders and Outsiders 19
Reflexivity: My Identity 22
Cooperative Advocacy 26
Relationship with the Field 28
Analysis and Critique 32

Chapter 3
Tawhid: Perfect Unity 35
Doctrine and History of *Tawhid* 36
Tawhid of Life 39
Tawhid of Society 40
Converts and *Tawhid* 42

Chapter 4
Umma: Perfect Community 47
Umma is a type of *Tawhid* 47
Social Unity over the Individual 49
Breakdown of the *Umma* 51
Freedom of Belief and Apostasy 53
Expectations of the New Umma 56

Chapter 5
A Perfect Dream 63
Christianity is a Known Element 63
The Attraction, not the Motivation 66
Westerners and Western Money: Missionaries and the Dream 68
Do No Harm 71
Anomie 73
Disappointment 77

Chapter 6
A Perfect Believer 79
Relating to Fellow Believers 80
Relating to the Community of One's Birth 85
Striving to be the Perfect Believer but Labelled a Deviant 87
A Believer Honouring the Family? Don't Ask Don't Tell 91
Demonstrating the Character of a Good Believer 93

Chapter 7
A Perfect Identity 97
Some Theories of Identity 97
Why Identity Matters 101
Adhesive Identities 103
Influences on Identity Development 110
Adaptation Processes 112

Chapter 8
Conclusion 115
Second-Generation Converts 115
Whose Risk? Whose Dream? 119

Bibliography 123
Index 139

Acknowledgements

This book is based on my PhD thesis and is possible thanks to the support of a wonderful network of people who have seen me through the process of studies, research and writing. While I am indebted to so many for their help with this project, most of them would prefer not to be named.

First and foremost, there are those who gave of their time to share their stories with me. There are also the *mutanasrin*, Arab Christians and missionaries who helped me to meet people, helped me to process what I was learning and helped me in the most practical of ways. Many of them also became good friends. I wish we lived in a world where it would be safe and wise to thank you all publicly, but as I cannot do so, I hope that you are aware of how much I appreciate your partnership and hope that we can own this research together.

There are a few people I can thank openly, though. It was a privilege to work under my supervisors at the University of Bristol: I am honoured by Tariq Modood's willingness to share of his valuable perspective and enormous experience with me, and I appreciate greatly Ruth Levitas's commitment to always pushing me to the highest of standards. They, along with my examiners Philip Lewis and Fiona Bowie, ensured that this study reflects a depth and detail of analysis of which I can stand proud. My parents, Larry and Stephanie Kraft, helped me in a variety of ways, ranging from travel companionship to copyediting; it was a rare privilege to work with them.

I also appreciate the friendships forged with my colleagues in the University of Bristol Sociology department, and my many other dear, dear friends in Bristol for their academic, emotional, spiritual and practical help and encouragement. The same goes to my friends in Brazil, the United States, Syria, Lebanon and elsewhere who are still a part of my life even after many years of physical distance... thanks to all many times over.

I am also grateful to the ORSAS, University of Bristol, and to Resound Corporation for their financial support which made this research possible.

More recently, I owe a debt of gratitude to Robin Wainwright for connecting me with Regnum Books and the Oxford Centre of Missions Studies. The support I have received from the people I met there, particularly David Singh who made sure this book became a reality, has been invaluable in the process of revisiting my research.

Acknowledgements

Introduction

I met my new friends at a bus stop a little ways up from my house. They had come all the way across town to meet me, but promised it wasn't out of their way. I exchanged cheek kisses with Noura[1] then shook her husband Abdel's hand. Once we had exchanged a full round of greetings, he said, "Let's go? The meeting starts in a few minutes and we don't want to be late!"

We walked back in the direction from which I'd come, passed my building, then turned left, up an alleyway and into the slum that sprawled behind my home. As we walked, we talked. I asked them how they were doing and what meetings they had been to lately. They chatted a little about their favourite gathering that week and then asked after my health and my research. Noura took my hand in hers and squeezed it, saying that they were praying for me as I did the Lord's work.

We can't have walked more than ten minutes when we stopped at a nondescript concrete building. We entered a dim hallway with peeling dark green paint and unfinished concrete stairs. Piles of muddy dust gathered in the corners of the tiny staircase. We headed up three stories, tiptoeing gingerly as we found our way in the dim light of a tiny skylight, then entered a two-room flat.

A young gentleman with streaks of gray in his hair, who introduced himself as Michael, stood to greet me. He informed me that they had been waiting: it was only at this point I learned that they did not have a regularly scheduled meeting on this day, that this was a special meeting arranged specifically to help with my research. He introduced me to the other people present. Two young women sat on ancient upholstered chairs to my right, and a student stood behind a swanky new musical keyboard. When Noura and Abdel saw the keyboard, they walked over to congratulate the young man on his new prize. He beamed his pleasure and played out a few bars to show off. A moment later, an older man wandered out of the kitchen, bearing tea. Michael informed me that this man was actually born into a Christian family but only recently became a believer. Everyone else present was born into Islam. As I may have guessed, he said, Michael was not his real name.

The group launched into a couple of enthusiastic, if off-tune, praise songs, enjoying the sound produced by the new keyboard, apparently without regard for the reaction of neighbours who might hear Christian music echoing around

[1] Any names used are changed.

this poor neighbourhood, not far from where certain infamous Islamic groups were said to have their base.

Then Michael greeted me again. He asked Abdel to introduce me and my project to the half dozen or so who had gathered with us, and they both reiterated that they were there to help me. They believe it is important for the story of the *mutanasrin*, the converts to Christ, to be known. They face many challenges and want help resolving those challenges, so they were ready to do whatever it might take to help me with my research.

During the next two hours, Michael did most of the talking, with the other members of his little flock occasionally contributing a thought. This is a new group, he explained. Except himself, Noura and Abdel, no one in the group had known Jesus for more than a year, and each person faced his/her unique challenges. One of the young women told me that she was a widow, living hundreds of miles away from her family, who had disowned her, but not before taking her baby away in order to raise the child as a Muslim. I already knew of the challenges Noura and Abdel had faced during the years that they each walked the path of an apostate alone, on the fine line between trying to please their families and dealing with the loneliness of rejection. I knew how much they were loving the freedom they now enjoyed in newlywed life, attending as many as a dozen Christian meetings each week, more than making up for lost time!

Michael then launched into a theoretical presentation with his analysis of the identity dynamics and challenges faced by converts. I nodded: he was repeating many of the things I'd heard before. But then I noticed that the rest of the room were staring at him, perplexed. They had not thought about analysing their situation. They had simply thought about how much they loved Jesus and occasionally wondered if life really had to be so hard. What Michael was telling me, gave them hope that perhaps it would not always be so difficult, that they had options.

When the meeting ended, the older, Christian-born gentleman insisted on having us all over to his neighbouring home for a special dinner, in my honour.

It is in honour of the hundreds, perhaps thousands, of groups such as these – individuals, families and groups in the Arab world who come from a Muslim background, but who have chosen to follow Christianity, or Christ – that I write the words that follow. May they continue facing their challenges with innocent hearts and with perseverance. But may others be available to help them in the ways that they need.

Background to the Topic

The idea for this research was borne out of a conversation I once had with a Muslim professor. He was proud to call himself a heretical Muslim who refused to follow the religion he inherited from his family, but he was a Muslim even so. I started telling him about a few conversations I had been having with people about conversion out of Islam, and he interrupted me, saying that conversion out of Islam does not exist. What ensued could best be described as a stare-down. He, the older, renowned academic, assuring me that once a Muslim always a Muslim. I, the younger student, informing him that I had in fact met people who had left Islam. We were at an impasse and after a few moments of mutual discomfort, moved on to a different topic.

After I left his office, I couldn't shake his reaction from my thoughts. This man was an internationally-renowned, widely-published academic who had travelled the world. He himself told me that he did not believe in the teachings of Islam. How could such an open-minded person refuse to believe in conversion?

I thought about some of the Christians I had met in the Middle East. There were, to be sure, many who agreed with my professor. But then there were those who told me that, while one might leave Islam, it is not desirable nor is it necessary. Rather, we should be telling Muslims about Jesus, or better yet *'Isa*, the name to which the Christ is referred in the Qur'an, and encourage them to follow him. Ideally, in those conversations we would use Qur'anic stories about Jesus and only occasionally reference the Bible. In this sense, they would not be leaving Islam. They can be like my professor, only instead of choosing to believe in nothing, they choose to believe in Jesus. My professor may have thought such an idea was ridiculous, but my Christian friends thought it made perfect sense.

But I'd also met a number of people who had left Islam, and by virtue of leaving Islam had left everything they had ever known, in order to become Christian. Many had been rejected by their families, disinherited. Quite a few had even moved to Europe or the United States seeking reprieve or refuge from the abuse and rejection they felt at home, because their community would not accept their rejection of Muslim-hood.

At the very least, it was clear that this was a topic that evoked strong emotions. I wanted to understand why. But I wanted more than that. I had met people, born in Muslim families, who wanted to believe in Jesus; I knew it was their decision and, as a Jesus-follower myself, I certainly did not want to undermine their decision. I wanted to know what I might do to support their needs. Is the correct response to tell them that Muslim heretical academics know best – that leaving Islam is an empirical impossibility? Or is the correct response to help them fill out their paperwork to apply for asylum in the West? Neither option resonated with me, nor with most of the Christians I knew.

As is true of most good research, I may have uncovered more questions than answers. This study provides insight into why this topic is so emotionally-charged, but does not present any formulaic solutions for moving beyond the emotions. It is my hope, however, that the insight provided here will help people who believe in the fundamental freedom of belief, to assist converts to enjoy their rights while living within the bounds of their consciences. I also hope that this can contribute to a thoughtful discussion about the dynamics of conversion, in which the lead role is played by those human beings living the experience of faith-change.

A Word on Terminology, Sociology and Conversion

From the beginnings of Sociology as a discipline, religion has been one of its central themes of study. Religion has always played a significant role in society's structure, functioning, activities and networks, and is also a defining element in the lives of individuals. Yet religion is a contentious concept, and it has long been difficult even for theorists to agree on so much as a definition (Mol 1976).

Émile Durkheim (d. 1917) was one of the early social theorists to directly take on the phenomenon of religion. He provided a helpful starting point in *The Elementary Forms of Religious Life* with a definition that has been debated and contested by sociologists of religion over the course of decades of religious study: "A religion is a unified system of beliefs and practices relative to sacred things, that is to say, things set apart and surrounded by prohibitions – beliefs and practices that unite its adherents in a single moral community called a church" (Durkheim 2001:46). I suggest that this definition contains too much detail for such a universal concept, since many movements or institutions may be considered religions that do not fit this definition precisely. However, it does set out some key components that may be said to characterise religion: *a set of beliefs, a social institution embodied in a community,* and *a sense of the sacred* (including, for many but not all, a supernatural). Different religious communities may emphasise different components differently, but most of what is called a "religion" will include these characteristics.

Sociology of Religion has developed mainly out of an interest in explaining or predicting the demise of religion as an important part of society, and when this did not happen, attempting to explain why.[2] As a result, religiosity has been critiqued and justified, but rarely described or analysed. In recent years, though, such a bias in the study of religion has diminished somewhat as more and more scholars have grown interested in understanding the lives and perspectives of people of faith for what they are, rather than for what they are not. Increasingly, religious converts are seen as active agents making their own choices about change (Smilde 2007:6-7). While many theorists are still primarily comparing religion with secularisation, others recognise that this focus has obscured many of the rich and significant changes happening in societies around the world, driven or inspired by religion, that do not fit into previous Western-centric models.[3]

---

[2] See, for example: Stark and Bainbridge 1985 and 1996, Davie 1994, Stark and Finke 2000, Reiss 2000, Heelas and Woodhead 2005

[3] See, for example: Bruce 1999, Lamb and Bryant 1999, Rambo 1999, Jenkins 2002, Beaman 2003, Chao 2006

In Sociology of Religion, conversion has received a fair bit of attention in a variety of different contexts.[4] While conversion is a very personally and historically situated concept, and therefore no single definition is likely to capture it, one useful broad definition is that it is "*a definite break with one's former identity such that the past and the present are antithetical in some important respects*" (Barker and Currie 1985:305; see also Travisano 1970). Conversion does not necessarily involve all aspects of religion as defined above: it may or may not involve beliefs, social institutions or sense of the sacred. Indeed, not all religious changing is necessarily conversion, and not all conversion is necessarily religious (Wohlrab Sahr 2006:74).

In fact, in some ways this study is not about conversion at all, since many Arabs of a Muslim background who follow a Christian faith might argue that they have not experienced that definite break with their former identity, rather that they have merely added to their existing sense of self. The term "conversion" is debated and can mean different things. This dynamic will be explored in later chapters, but all participants in this study did experience at least some degree of change and break with the past, so based on a loose interpretation of the above definition, I do consider that this is a study of "converts" (though, when referring to individuals in the analysis, I try to respect their self-identification, whether as convert, Christian, follower of Christ, Muslim-Background Believer (MBB), Believer of a Muslim Background (BMB), or something else).

It is easy to investigate conversion as a phenomenon that occurs to people, but I have found it to be of key importance to approach conversion from the situated perspective of those being studied, as active agents, rather than referring to converts as passive participants in their own life processes (Smilde 2007). Conversion studies have increasingly tended to study conversion as a process, not a moment (Van Nieuwkerk 2006b:11), investigating questions of identity, lifestyle, community and relationships among converts – things that are directly relevant to their lived experience – more than reasons why people change religions (Carrothers 2010:151). This is what this study seeks to do.

Defining and categorising converts has also been a focus of conversion studies. Some categorisations of converts bear mentioning. One important

---

[4] Conversion theory has been an ongoing and popular field of inquiry in various different disciplines of the social sciences and has undergone a series of different variations and emphases. In his discussion of conversion literature, Henri Gooren pointed out some of the main ongoing weaknesses of conversion studies, among these: that the focus has been almost entirely on conversion within Christianity or to New Religious Movements, in the United States and Europe, and that there has been little investigation into why people disaffiliate from religious groups, that is, little investigation into what happens post-conversion (Gooren 2007:347). More recent studies of conversion have been less deterministic, looking at conversion as a broader social phenomenon, and taking the distinct beliefs of different religious traditions into consideration when investigating faith-changers.

distinction is between the institutional and spiritual convert (Zinnbauer and Pargament 1998). There are various ways of phrasing this distinction. Travisano (1970) famously described the distinction as between "conversion" and "alteration", but regardless of how it is worded, there is an important difference between the individual who converts because of convenience in institutional affiliation with a different group, and the individual who undergoes a radical change in worldview because of a new understanding of, or encounter with, the sacred. Though there are a few participants in this study who told me they converted for more institutional reasons, the overwhelming majority prefer to see themselves as having experienced a deep spiritual change (in some cases without an accompanying institutional affiliation), so this study somewhat bears more relevance to spiritual converts (those who have experienced, in Travisano's language, an alteration). As we will see, though, such a categorisation is problematic, since the institutional and spiritual changes experienced by the participants in this study are closely connected. This complicates attempts to distinguish between institutional and spiritual motivations.

Another distinction between converts is that between relational and rational converts (van Nieuwkerk 2006b:3), or people who conceive of their change in terms of creed or doctrinal conviction, as opposed to those who see their change primarily as a result of significant relationships. This project included both relational and rational converts, though all stories involved an element of each, and found that regardless of how they came to their decision they faced many of the same challenges in community and identity definition.

Conversion from a Muslim background to a Christian faith is often considered "apostasy".[5] Though few participants in this study would refer to themselves as apostates, an argument can be, and at times has been, made that they all are. Studies of apostasy out of Islam have highlighted the importance placed on loyalty to Islam and the worldwide Muslim community, especially within the framework of honour and shame and Islam's reputation, an issue of key importance to this study.

Background: Why Do People Convert?

There are usually two distinct processes in a conversion from a Muslim background to a Christian faith: rejection of Islam and an embracing of

[5] Most sociological studies of Muslim apostasy have focused on acts of defiance against Islam by Muslims or former Muslims – acts that may also be labelled blasphemy. The Rushdie affair, in which Salman Rushdie's book was taken to be highly offensive of Islam – even more so because the author was of a Muslim background – inspired extensive academic analysis of Islam and apostasy in and following the early 1990s. See, for example: Slaughter 1993, Werbner 1996, Ahmed 2003

Christian beliefs. Studies of conversion to Islam[6] have also identified rejection and adoption as essential and distinct processes, in terms of both the faith abandoned and the faith adopted. Stefano Allievi, for example, argues that asking "Why does someone convert?" is not even useful, as it does not look at the essential issues involved. Instead, he recommends asking, "Why does someone convert to a specific religion?" This question leads the researcher to explore what people are converting from and why they started looking for a new religion, as well as how they choose the system to which they are converting (Allievi 2002). I may add that it is also imperative to consider the cultural and social context in which the conversion takes place.

Research data on conversions to Islam suggest that the process is anticipated by an individual determining that his/her religion of origin, and the values of his/her parents and society, are irrelevant. One common path involves the following: a decision to abandon one's heritage (usually Christianity), followed by a period of time in which the individual avoids any spiritual activity or interest. After several years, when s/he begins to ask existential questions or has an emotional experience that causes renewed interest in religion or spirituality, s/he looks to a new religious framework, something different from that which s/he already rejected (Bourque 2006). Similarly, researchers focusing on other religious traditions also found that conversion to a different, mainstream religious group often requires a deliberate renouncing of previous faith(s) or, at least, intense disillusionment with the previous situation (Iannacone 1995:291, Jindra 2011:296).

Participants in this study all had different stories. Some had never known much about Islam to start with, or had always been somewhat disinterested. Others had previously been very devout Muslims, even, in some cases, extremists. Those who had previously believed in Islam had either rejected those beliefs before taking interest in a new set of beliefs, or been through a process of rejecting Islam as they decided to follow this new faith. But all of them had rejected Islam as a set of beliefs and told me that this was an important part of their conversion story.

In a long, constantly evolving history of conversion studies, one conclusion about the motivations behind conversion seems to continually thrive. In the words of seminal conversion theorists Stark and Finke, "Conversion is seldom about seeking or embracing an ideology; it is about bringing one's religious behavior into alignment with that of one's friends and family members" (Stark and Finke 2000:117). That is, when attachments to members become stronger than attachments to nonmembers, it becomes more socially expedient to join the group, regardless of whether those relationships, or doctrinal conviction, or

[6] Conversion from a Christian background to a Muslim faith has received quite a bit more academic attention than conversion out of Islam, the focus of this study, but there are some useful parallels and comparisons that can be drawn from the literature on conversion to Islam.

other influences, were what first drew their attention to the new group. The convert is seen as playing both a passive role, influenced by various constraints and pressures, and also an active role, pursuing the affiliation to which s/he can best relate; social relationships are essential to this process (Jindra 2011). Conversely, conversion, especially when into a faith not accepted by the broader community, is more likely when people lack sufficient attachments with people who would hold them back from such a choice, and when they have something to gain from the deviant act.[7]

This emphasis on social ties, however, is lacking in that it does not allow for secret conversion: many Muslims have, knowing that their decision was socially deviant in their communities, changed beliefs in private and only informed a small and select group of people, sometimes years after they made their decision to change. They see their conversion moment as the moment they changed beliefs, not the moment their change became known in a social context.

So, social ties do not necessarily seem to be the most important draw to a Christian faith. They do, however, help explain where people get the idea of changing their beliefs in the first place, especially for women. Helen Rose Ebaugh expressed well the simultaneously social and personal nature of the process in describing how Catholic nuns came to the decision to leave the convent: "While the decision to exit is a very personal one, it is inevitably made in a social context and is highly influenced by the reactions of other people" (Ebaugh 1988:108). Many, though not all, female converts from a Muslim background to a Christian faith, could identify with such a statement. In keeping with Feminist theory, it may be expected that women might approach their faith and also tell their stories in terms of relationships, more so than men.

Many women come to consider Christianity when they fall in love with a Christian man. In Islamic law, a Muslim man is allowed to marry a Christian woman while the reverse is not allowed, largely because of rules and traditions of patrilineality which ensure that the children of a Muslim man will be Muslim. It is not uncommon for Muslim women who fall in love with Christian men to consider adopting the men's Christian faith. Their union is not allowed in Islam, nor is it legal in most Arab countries; in fact, if a Muslim woman, or a Muslim convert to Christianity, manages to marry a Christian man (either illegally or in a country where their union is allowed), her marriage to a Christian may be seen as an act of apostasy in and of itself, regardless of her personal faith decision. Nonetheless, those women who choose to change faith as a result of their relationships with Christian men try to minimise the significance of the relationship and emphasise the course of their own beliefs, even if relationships were certainly significant in their process. Many women

---

[7] See Stark and Finke 2000:117-118, Downes and Rock 2003:25, Cao et al 2010 for further discussion of the relationship between social structure and deviance

also change after close family members choose to follow Christianity. Other women have Christian friends who start evangelising them, and their interest is piqued.

While some men share similar stories, there are many Muslim men who pursue a Christian faith on apparently entirely individual lines. In my research, I did not meet any men who believed after falling in love with a Christian woman, for example. I did, however, meet several who converted before knowing any other people who shared their new faith. Many of these men said they became interested in Christianity because they listened to an evangelistic radio station or because they came across a Bible which attracted their interest. Some of these men found a Bible in a social context, such as a student who was required to read it for his university course; others pursued Bible reading more independently, such as a man who simply picked it up at a bookstore. Regardless, these mens' stories indicated very little influence of relationships or social networks in their faith decision.

Ultimately, most conversions involve both relationships and ideological change, in varying proportions. In this study, the premise about social ties held true if the concept of relationships is broadened to include other types of emotional attachment. For example, some people told me that they had many questions and studied the two religions extensively, but did not decide until they had a dream which convinced them or until they were emotionally touched in a relationship with a Christian. Other emotional experiences might include an employment or educational opportunity which is attributed to supernatural means, witnessing a miracle, or having a dream. For example, one participant told me that a voice told him to go apply to take an entrance exam for further education, against his father's will and without having prepared for the exam. He passed the exam. This man had no previous knowledge of Christianity, but he sensed this miracle was from Christ, and so he started telling people about Christianity. When he finally did meet a priest, he realised that what he had been preaching was in fact Christian doctrine, and he was eventually baptised in an Orthodox Christian church. His story is particularly dramatic, but illustrates well how someone's devotion to Christianity can be entirely founded in emotional attachment, albeit with an understanding of and adherence to Christian doctrine following.[8]

Others said that they were very attracted to a church community, or had some spiritual experience, but that they were also convinced of its doctrinal truth before they made a definite decision to follow Christianity. I met several individuals whose stories started with meeting a Christian who became a good and respected friend. As the friendship developed, they tried to convince their friend to become Muslim but failed; instead, they began to wonder about, even

[8] This confluence of emotional and intellectual change is a theme in much sociological literature on conversion. For more on the topic, see: Stark and Bainbridge 1985, Rothbaum 1988, Yang 1999, Roald 2006

envy, what the other person believed. In another scenario, one young man told me that his process of change began when he came across on-line chat rooms for dialogue between Islam and Christianity. He took it upon himself to defend Islam, while finding himself more and more attracted to what he was learning about Christianity. He started reading avidly about Christ and Christianity, but he did not make a decision until he personally met a Christian who introduced him to other Christian believers; he also had three dreams in which he saw Jesus talking to him. In such stories, people's interest begins with an intellectual curiosity and their decision is solidified with an emotional connection. Most people I met had an emotional experience, such as a dream or a personal connection with a Christian, before actually making a faith change. Each story was slightly different, but they all involved both emotions and intellect.

Why leave Islam? There is an emotional element, as often as not related to strained family relationships or discontent. There is also an intellectual element. Regardless, most converts gave up on Islam long before considering an alternate faith and some never reached a point of firmly believing in their family's religion in the first place. Why embrace a Christian faith? First, because they have rejected Islam. Second, in response to both an emotional and an intellectual pull.

Context

This study refers to a phenomenon that is happening transnationally, across the Arab world, but I focus on the Middle East, where there is a historical Christian minority and a Muslim (mostly Sunni but not exclusively) majority. When I first set out on this research project, my intention had been to focus this study specifically in the countries of the Middle East (Lebanon, Syria, Iraq, Jordan, Palestine, Egypt), and perhaps only two or three of those nations, so I attended a gathering of North Africans (Libyans, Tunisians, Algerians, Moroccans, Mauritanians) simply for exposure to another part of the Arab world. However, I discovered there that the movement of conversions of people from a Muslim background to a Christian faith is not divided along national lines. I met Egyptians and Lebanese who are working in Morocco or Tunisia, for example, and I met North Africans who had studied in the Middle East. Later, through attending Internet chat meetings, I discovered a diaspora of Arab individuals who still have close ties to their home communities, by virtue of the ease of communication over the Internet and the ability to travel regularly. Many of the people with whom I interacted in this study were using programmes like Skype, MSN messenger and PalTalk to meet other converts or maintain friendships with people living abroad. This was in 2005-2007, and global connectivity has only increased since then.

Therefore, I decided to approach this study as an endeavour to understand something that is happening across a transnational community. Because there has been so little research published on the effects that apostasy, or conversion to a different faith, has on Arab Muslims, much less those who choose a Christian faith, I decided that, at this point, the most valuable contribution to understanding the consequences of such a decision would be to investigate this in its transnational setting, even though I still did focus on two countries: Lebanon and Egypt.

I chose Lebanon as a first site of research partly because I had lived there before: I did my MA at the American University of Beirut. I had made a number of friends in different Christian circles, including Lebanese Christians and foreign missionaries. I also had some friends who were converts. In a region where I knew trust relationships would be an important starting point, my ties to Lebanon could facilitate finding participants there using snowball sampling. In Lebanon there is no real government pressure against religious conversion, so security concerns regarding meeting converts were not what they are in other countries. This also means that there are a number of Arabs resident in Lebanon who are known as Muslim in their own countries but as Christian in Lebanon, including many students at Protestant seminaries. For these reasons, Lebanon was a natural starting place.

Lebanon is the Arab country with the strongest heritage of a Christian minority; when it was established as a nation with the help of the French in the 1930s, strongest political power was given to the Maronite Christian community, which was then a majority of the country's population.[9] This religious differentiation and preference is written into the Lebanese constitution: in fact the entire government structure is confessional, which means it is based on religious sectarianism. While this has contributed to much of the tension in Lebanon over the years, especially the sectarian tension which highlighted most of the Lebanese Civil War that ran from 1975 to 1990, it has also meant that Lebanon has been very open to Western influence and to values of individual freedom. Lebanon has been seen by many Arabs as a safe haven from the repressive governments and religious systems of their own countries. Nonetheless, communitarian religious loyalty is of paramount importance in a country where religious affiliation implies political loyalty. Though religious converts in Lebanon are relatively free from any sort of official pressure, communal pressure can be significant and even life-threatening for some.

Egypt was my second destination. It is the Arab country with the largest number of Christians, even though Christians constitute less than 10% of the country's total population (actual official figures do not exist as far as I could discover). Egyptian Christians are very active, both socially and religiously, and there are frequent evangelistic campaigns and conferences held in Egypt.

---

[9] The majority is now Muslim. Exact figures are unknown since there has not been a national census for eight decades, but estimates are that Shi'a Islam is the largest group, followed by Sunni Islam. Christians probably comprise approximately 30% of the population.

These are usually by Christians and for Christians, mostly Egyptians but also from other Arab nations. Additionally, Egypt has attracted a great deal of missionary activity, and Egyptian converts have successfully networked with both missionaries and international human rights networks. For these reasons, and also because I had a few good contacts there, Egypt was a natural choice for my second destination. In fact, for people involved in work with Arab converts, considering the size and vocality of communities of converts in Egypt, it seemed essential that I visit Egypt in a study of the transnational movement of Muslims to a Christian faith. Prestigious institutions of higher education in Egypt also hosted a number of students from Arab countries at the time of my field research, so I met not only Egyptians but some converts from other countries while there.

Several Egyptian participants explained to me the strong intellectual heritage that has inspired a deep passion that I found among many Egyptians. Much of the greatest Arab literature in the last century, ranging from works of fiction to Islamic philosophy, has come out of Egypt. Al-Azhar, the most famous Islamic university in Cairo, is considered the forefront of Muslim thought in many Muslim circles. While Egypt is possibly the Arab country which is seeing the largest number of people converting from Islam to a Christian faith, it may also be the Arab country in which converts suffer the most for their decision. There have been frequent court cases in Egypt regarding conversion and religious identity.[10] Since the 2011 revolution, as of this writing it seems that tensions between Christians and Muslims have further intensified.

In the light of my choice to focus on conversions across the Arab world, a constant methodological challenge I faced, especially in the analysis, was to build on the similarities between different countries while acknowledging the cultural differences between the various contexts. However, this was as true within any one country as it was between countries. For example, among Lebanese, the religious attitudes of interviewees who had lived through the Lebanese war (1975-1990) were remarkably different from those of people who were too young to remember, or who had lived abroad at the time. In Egypt, I quickly recognised a distinction between people from Upper Egypt, which in some ways is culturally more like Sudan or other sub-Saharan nations,

[10] Among noteworthy cases, prior to the 2011 Revolution, included daughters of a Coptic Christian who had changed his government registration to "Muslim" for reasons of expediency but who were as a result unable to marry Christian men because their government identification labelled them as Muslim women (in most Arab countries a Muslim woman cannot legally marry a Christian man, though the reverse is allowed); a Baha'i family that wanted their religion acknowledged, since at present they are seen as Muslim apostates, because Baha'i is not accepted as a religion by Egyptian authorities; and a Muslim blogger who was arrested for openly challenging al-Azhar University, calling for a reform of Islam. Little changed after the revolution, other than a potentially slower response from the government bureaucracy.

and people from Cairo, in Lower Egypt, which is much more urbanised and intellectual. Therefore, not only between countries, but between backgrounds, working with such a hugely diverse community of people meant that my analysis needed to always be sensitive to the distinctiveness of each individual's background. Sometimes the differences are explicitly stated in my analysis; other times, they are reflected more subtly according to people's interaction in a given situation.

Nonetheless, my research base is defined broadly because members of the researched community define themselves that way, whether they have had an opportunity to meet Arab MBBs in other countries or regions, or not. I met individuals who have invested significant time in initiatives to facilitate regular contact for converts all across the Arab world, and I learned of international events for Arab converts. Almost all the individuals I met who attended these events told me of their appreciation for the opportunity to spend time with people "like them" (a phrase converts often used to refer to each other). In fact, for many, their community is limited to people from Arab countries merely because of linguistic limitations – they would like to include and spend time with converts out of Islam in non-Arab nations as well. Since their definition of their community spanned the Arab world, that is how I have defined it as well.

Summary of Methodology

Over the course of an intensive three year period (2005-2007), in addition to extended stays of approximately two months each in Lebanon and Egypt, I also did on-line research, both in chat rooms and via email conversations with converts, and met with Arab MBBs at conferences and on shorter trips to various Arab countries. Though I spent most of my field research time in the Middle East, I met with individuals from most countries of the Arab world, except for the Gulf region. This omission mainly reflects the political and societal forces working against converts in the Gulf region being known openly or having any contact with a foreigner (non-Arab), as opposed to a deliberate research strategy.

There is no knowledge of how many converts there are in the Arab world, as it is almost entirely an underground movement. Without concrete quantitative data, I am limited in the claims I can make in this study, and I recognise that my data may not be representative of this community (Jacobsen and Landau 2003:190). Though I would have liked to have done a quantitative study to produce a valid estimate of the size and demographics of this community, that was not feasible: such an undertaking would be logistically impractical and highly security-sensitive. Even so, the questions on which I chose to focus, which I believe are the most urgent with regard to understanding this movement, are best analysed qualitatively.

My methods of data collection were unstructured interviews with a number of converts in the tradition of narrative research, and ethnographic research which included participant observation at gatherings of converts and more casual conversations with members of the community and people who know them. In doing ethnographic research, I was largely seeking to understand what life is like for a convert, identify the issues that MBBs face on a regular basis, and further investigate those issues. The interviews were an opportunity to pursue those same questions in more depth. Combining the ethnographic fieldwork with narrative interviews helped construct stories of the experiences of converts, and a larger story of the context in which conversion happens, with an understanding of the dynamics surrounding their narratives (Gubrium and Holstein 2008:249).

I chose a very open-ended narrative interview style, in which participants were asked to tell about their spiritual journeys. Though I did probe and insert questions throughout their narratives, I mostly allowed participants to talk uninterruptedly about their experiences, a process by which I could participate with them in making sense of their experiences as they talked (Jindra 2011:278). I found that most of the topics I wanted to cover in the interview had been talked through by the end of their stories, and I asked a few follow-up questions afterwards. Topics covered included: how and why they decided to (or not to) tell their families about their conversion and their relationship to their families since, their relationships with other friends from before, whether and how they discuss religion with Muslims, their fears, their religious practices and how they have changed, their opinion of the Qur'an and Islam, how they have approached questions of marriage and child-rearing, any legal hassles they have faced, how their decision has affected their careers, their opinion of foreign missionaries, what terms they use to identify themselves, and their opinion about their religious registration with the government. Based on a grounded theory approach, I allowed themes for investigation to emerge from the data collection process (Charmaz 2008): as participants told me of issues that were important to them, I would often add them to the interview schedule, and as they expressed a lack of interest in other questions, I would emphasise those less in later interviews.

I conducted formal interviews with most of the research participants. Of 33 formal interviews, 18 were in Egypt and 15 in Lebanon; 16 were with women and 17 with men; most participants ranged in age from their early twenties to mid-thirties (with the exception of five individuals in their forties or fifties); they came from five different Arab countries (to remain unnamed for security reasons); most had converted within the last 10 years but 9 had converted more than 10 years previously. No further demographic data will be provided out of respect for the need to protect many of their identities.

Besides the people with whom I conducted formal interviews, there were also several individuals who contributed to the body of data through conversations in an ongoing friendship, brief informal interviews (by which I mean scenarios such as a fifteen minute conversation with someone who was introduced to me by a mutual friend because his/her story was relevant to my study), or through their participation in a fellowship group that I visited in-person or online. In both Lebanon and Egypt, as well as in other gatherings of converts, I spent time doing participant observation in Christian gatherings that had several, or only, MBB participants. These visits and more informal conversations took place not only on my field research trips, but at conferences and during informal visits to friends, both in the Middle East and in the UK.

I met the research participants through a wide variety of networks and gatekeepers. Some were friends of mine before I began this project; others I met through the introduction of a mutual friend. I also networked with some organisations that work with Christians and converts in the Arab world. The greatest challenge I faced in building my research sample was gaining access to as diverse a group of converts as possible. I found that through any one gatekeeper I was able to meet a number of people who had many shared experiences, but s/he was often reluctant or unable to introduce me to converts in different groups. So I devoted a good bit of effort to connecting with as many different groups of converts, Arab Christians and missionaries, as possible, in each country.

In both Lebanon and Egypt, but especially in Egypt, it took most of the duration of my time in-country to find participants of a different socioeconomic background from the majority of the people I interviewed; had I stayed longer I could have met more people from less educated or more Islamically-conservative communities, for example. In addition, based on information shared with me by participants and gatekeepers, I concluded that there are a number of converts who are much more integrated in their Muslim communities and who are particularly reluctant to have anything to do with outsiders, especially foreigners. I had very little contact with people who fit that description. Bearing in mind these restraints to finding a truly representative sample, I believe that I did meet a variety of different people, from several different Arab countries and different socioeconomic backgrounds. Within this sample, a number of themes emerged that are likely relevant to the reality of most converts in the Arab world. Nonetheless, further ethnographic exploration is warranted.

The formal interviews were conducted mainly in Arabic but also often in English. If the participant was an English speaker, s/he could choose to talk in English, Arabic, or a bit of each.[11] Sometimes communication was difficult because of linguistic confusion, particularly when people spoke rural dialects, but language differences did not tend to be prohibitive. Early on in my experience of conducting qualitative research in the Arab world, I learned to be just as suspicious of recording devices as were most of my informants. Cultural and political factors, combined with a general preference for a conversation between people rather than with a machine, have ensured that I can obtain

[11] Though I am fluent in Arabic, some contacts preferred to translate from rural dialects to English than to an Arabic dialect with which I was more comfortable

much better data when no recording equipment is present. The sensitivity of this research topic meant that this decision was all the more important. Instead, I took copious notes and wrote up my memory of the interview, word for word, as soon as the interview was over. Sometimes, even a notebook was too sensitive, in which case I would run to my computer as soon as possible after the interview ended and write down as much as I could remember. Fortunately, my memory was good: while these transcripts were not always word-for-word, in those instances that I could later show them to the participants for feedback, they confirmed that I had mostly captured the interview. Also, due to the sensitivity of the research, as well as cultural suspicions of a paper trail, I did not ask participants for written consent, rather depended on verbal informed consent following a detailed description of the research which I gave them before beginning the interview.

During many interviews there was a third party present, sometimes to help aid communication between dialects or translating to English, and sometimes simply in the role of a trusted mutual friend. I usually found the presence of a third party to be beneficial, since the person present would be someone known and trusted by the participant, who would already know most of what the interviewee was telling me. Furthermore, whenever possible, I interviewed couples together. The presence of a mutual friend often helped to build trust quickly and develop a comfortable rhythm of conversation. Once in a while, though, when the third person left the room, the interviewee would tell me a secret, and I tried to make sure there was always an opportunity to share things more privately if s/he felt the need. I explained to interviewees my commitment to keeping their narratives fully in confidence, but only occasionally did individuals share with me things that they did not want their trusted friends to know.

Organisation of Chapters

In the following chapter, I explore the actual research process more in depth. The approach I took to the research and the role played by the researched group themselves are an important part of the study, indeed they are somewhat inseparable from the findings, so this relationship deserves careful consideration.

The rest of the book explores the lives, cultures and values of converts from an Arab Muslim background. Each chapter will look at a different piece of "heaven" they are searching for as they live their lives in their new faith. Chapters 3 and 4 investigate the communities, values and mindset that many converts are coming from, framing the discussion around two Islamic doctrines: *tawhid* (unity) and *umma* (community). Chapters 5-7 investigate the dreams MBBs have for their new lives: the preexisting image of Christianity that they bring into conversion, the community they are looking for, and the identity they are seeking to develop.

Each chapter talks about a dream, or an aspect of "heaven in the real world", because an underlying theme of this discussion is the expectations and ideals which need to be negotiated and tempered as someone adjusts to a convert identity. As this adjustment takes shape, dreams are reformulated in the wake of acute disappointment. What remains is an acceptance of the challenges and of faith for what it is, and yet, continued hope for something better to come.

The Perfect Researcher

In many ways, I was and continue to be inseparable from this research. Research with vulnerable or stigmatised populations demands a particularly thoughtful level of consideration for questions of integrity and ethics, and a sensitivity to the unique context being studied (Benson and Thomas 2010:679-680). The process of reflecting carefully on my research practice became an integral part of the data collection and analysis process. As I consider the research and the researcher in this chapter, I am equally considering the researched community.

This study is, to some extent, as much about me as it is about the community researched. In my attempt to understand intimately and portray accurately the community of converts in the Arab world, I needed to build a strong trust relationship with members of that community. I appeared in their lives for a short season, but during that time I journeyed with them and sought ways to ensure that the relationship did not end at the completion of my field research. Their willingness to share with me was based on trust and their understanding of who I am: what they shared and how they shared it was in response to their perceptions of our relationship. This chapter will explore some of those perceptions and expectations that the MBB community had of me, a researcher, which in turn framed the actual findings. I suggest that this was the appropriate way to conduct sensitive research of this sort and defend the integrity of my findings, even while issuing a call for other researchers to explore similar questions from their equally unique standpoints.

Insiders and Outsiders

Research in the social sciences, especially ethnographic research on a distant culture, is often defined as research of the "other". In many ways that is how this project could be described and will be seen, since I conducted this research as a part of my doctoral work for a British academic institution, and since I am an American studying a minority community in the Arab world.

Anthropologist Clifford Geertz wrote extensively about the endeavour to understand the world from the perspective of the "other". The goal of cultural "translation", he wrote, "is not a simple recasting of others' ways of putting things in terms of our own ways of putting them (that is the kind in which things get lost), but displaying the logic of their ways of putting them in the locutions of ours..." (Geertz 1983:10). We seek to bring ourselves and the "others" as close together as possible, but with full acceptance that this is one of those goals that can never be fully achieved. "We" will never be "them". Informants are not likely to welcome an outsider's attempts to try to become an insider, and furthermore, an ethnographer's job is to organise the experiences of those being studied in such a way as to make sense in the world of somewhat distant social scientific concepts (Geertz 1983:58).

I learned early on in my residence in the Middle East that the foreigner who thinks s/he will become an insider in the Arab world will be inevitably disappointed. Similarly, the ethnographer who thinks that s/he will become an insider is deceiving him/herself, and that should not even be the goal. While this represents a realistic attitude on the part of anthropologists, it is somewhat controversial because it suggests that the ethnographer must always study people who are the "other" – somehow exotic to him/her (Pease 2012:71-72).

The argument that an insider might have more difficulty than an outsider being objective when analysing a community (Jarvie 1969:506), is a common premise in social methodological writing, and in some ways, I saw how it applied to this research. It is not a straightforward conclusion, though, and many native researchers contest it as an assumption.

Linda Tuhiwai Smith, in her compelling discussion of indigenous research, describes some of the special challenges that native researchers face, as well as some of the benefits that they enjoy. Many indigenous groups are suspicious of the research enterprise in general because of centuries of treatment as the "other" by colonialists, missionaries and anthropologists, and abuse suffered in the process. Even so, they know that research and the knowledge it produces may be beneficial and so assent to being researched, but they may express a preference for non-indigenous researchers, albeit for, she argues, the wrong reasons. Sometimes in-group suspicion is greater than that of outsiders, and indigenous researchers are working in the midst of long-term relationships which extend beyond a research relationship, because they involve their families, communities, organisations, and local networks. Actually, though, this relational integration of native researchers can be seen as advantageous: "indigenous methodologies tend to approach cultural protocols, values and behaviours as an integral part of methodology" (Smith 1999:15), in a way that outsiders often do not have to consider. "'Who' is doing the writing is important in the politics of peoples; it is even more important in the politics of how these worlds are being represented 'back to' the West" (Smith 1999:37). Smith also recognises, though, that no indigenous researcher is fully an insider because the researcher role requires taking a somewhat removed perspective and a high degree of reflexivity.

Based on my experience in this project, I suggest that defining researchers as insiders or as outsiders is largely a futile endeavour and, therefore, researching the "other" also draws an unnecessary and artificial line between researcher and researched. If the researcher is fully an outsider, there will be no understanding upon which to build the research schedule: some common understanding is needed as a starting point. On the other hand, as Smith suggests, the moment an insider becomes the researcher, s/he is no longer truly an insider. Inevitably, the lines are blurred. My position in this research was certainly as an outsider, but there were elements in which I became an insider, which were crucial for the effective development of this project.

Since the members of the community researched in this study had a specific understanding of who was "like them", there was also a sense in which the distinction between an insider and an outsider was rather clearly defined. An insider seemed to be defined simply as *any Arabic-speaking individual from a Muslim background who chose (or whose family chose) to follow a Christian faith.* I met some non-Arabic speaking converts from Islam, either from other Muslim countries or who were raised in other parts of the world; they were warmly accepted by MBBs, but not necessarily granted insider status.

In many parts of the Middle East, there is an historic Arab Christian community, and members of those churches, even those who are devout in their Christian faith, are certainly not seen as MBB insiders. Some of them dedicate significant time and energy to working with individuals of a Muslim background, accepting the unique cultural situation of converts: those individuals are accepted as sympathisers, similar to Goffman's conception of the "wise" (Goffman 1963:41) that I will explore more in chapter 6. Though not an Arab, I was placed in roughly the same category. Actually, as a foreigner, a number of insiders actually trusted me more than they would an Arab Christian, especially as individuals got to know me better. Because of historic inter-religious tensions in the Middle East, some converts told me that they prefer to trust foreign Christians over Arab Christians.

Sharing a faith with the research community actually did give me an element of insider status. My relationship to the converts was strongly influenced by the fact that I would attend church and other meetings with them, pray with them, and join them in theological discussions. The fact that I spoke Arabic and had lived in the Middle East for several years also contributed to common ground. A person who was not an "insider" in the faith could probably never have done this research, because the group would only allow "full" insiders or sympathisers like myself, people who shared a Christian faith, into their trusted circle.

While I was more qualified as an insider than, for example, an Arab who did not share the participants' faith, or a foreign Christian who had no knowledge of the Arab world, I still was well aware of the limitations that my outsider status brought to this project. The circle of insiders is so specifically delineated, and many insiders are distinctly suspicious of outsiders, specifically because they have felt like other Christians have often taken advantage of them. For these reasons, there were many moments at which I thought it would be better for someone who was more of an insider to do this research than me. In fact, there were many members of the community to whom I was not able to gain access because I was an outsider.

As my field research continued, though, I came to discover reasons why it would be extremely difficult for a convert to study his/her context with much objectivity. This research investigates an underground community, largely considered deviant in its society, for which people have given their hearts and lives, often sacrificing comforts, relationships and more. Coming out of that experience, it is virtually impossible to objectively analyse the lives of other people who share that experience. One woman convert who helped me with logistics in the field had some research experience. Sometimes during an interview she would jump in to explain what participants were saying because she thought it was obvious, or make assumptions about what they were saying based on her own experiences. The more we worked together, the less she inserted her own preconceptions, but this would be a constant tendency the more shared experiences one had with the researched; such a temptation was more easily avoided for me, a relative outsider.

Reflexivity: My Identity

In order to be continually sensitive to the various expectations and pressures of my fieldwork with such a sensitive group, I found that I had to be constantly questioning and aware of my own position in the research. Reflexivity, a recognition that the researcher is inevitably a participant in the process, has become the bread and butter of qualitative research. It has also been contested for subjectivising research and putting the researcher into a position of privilege whereby the researcher becomes the focus of attention (Livholts 2012:4, Pease 2012:74). Perhaps the importance and type of reflexivity varies from one context to another: in this study, I found that a high degree of reflexivity was essential for conducting an inquiry and for ensuring I was appropriately sensitive to the vulnerabilities that the researched community face.

First, it was important that I consider what I was learning, hearing and seeing according to the context of my own position within the MBB community (Bhattacharya 2008:303-304). For example, there was an assumption among many participants that I did not understand their cultural situation, and so they treated the interview more as a cultural lesson for me (often, though not always, explaining things about Arab culture with which I was already familiar), than as a discussion of their own experiences within that cultural setting. When I was probing them on a detail of their account, it was not uncommon for them to take that as a lack of general knowledge, rather than a desire to understand more thoroughly their unique situation.

I came to realise, though, that the frustration of feeling that participants thought I knew nothing was actually an advantage, because it was far preferable to the alternative, that is, statements which they just assumed I understood. That would have been the tendency of many insiders being interviewed by cultural insiders. There is indeed a place for talking to members of researched communities as if we know nothing about their world. "What one may know as a researcher does not make one an expert in the eyes of respondents. The researcher asks respondents to be project consultants and is honest about his or her dependence on them and readiness to listen" (Bowser and Sieber 1993:169). This is especially important because the subjects of research often find it arrogant when outsiders act like they already know the culture they are studying perfectly well. I found that humility was the most appropriate approach to my research situation, as well, yielding the most useful results.

I was also in a unique position in terms of power relationships. Smith argues that a researcher needs to always recognise the power dynamic in research with minorities or across cultures. "Researchers are in receipt of privileged information... They have the power to distort, to make invisible, to overlook, to exaggerate and to draw conclusions, based not on factual data, but on assumptions, hidden value judgments, and often downright misunderstandings. They have the potential to extend knowledge or to perpetuate ignorance" (Smith 1999:176). Because any researcher can fall into this trap, there is a benefit to researching from a subordinate position, so that the researcher's power is no greater than it must be.

Being a Western foreigner who was born into a Christian family, there was some sense among many of the participants that I was coming from a dominant position. Certainly a history of abuses at the hands of missionaries and colonialists, and more recent experiences with missionaries who, in the opinion of many converts, use their access to financial resources to regulate converts' activities and efforts, contribute to this opinion about Westerners. The fact that the Arab Christian church has access to many more resources, especially from abroad, than do most converts, also adds to a sense of perceived inferiority. Though such dynamics may invoke a desire to try to become an equal in relation to the group being studied, feminist researchers are quick to point out that this is never truly possible, particularly when power relationships are involved. Just being another woman is not enough: there is racial and class tension, as well, or simply the sense of authority that one senses in response to the researcher's connection to an academic institution (Edwards 1993:187-189).

I found that many converts were actually well-practised at struggling against any sense of intimidation by Western Christians. In fact, their external demeanour toward me sometimes indicated that they believed, or were at least determined to convince me, that they were the ones in the position of superiority over me – although it is likely that for many participants this was a practised defense mechanism rather than an actual sense of authority.

On the other hand, gender and age are important definers of rank in many Middle Eastern communities, so being a young woman did significantly decrease my power position. In reflecting on my time in the field, I conclude that there is a sense in which the participants' emphasis on my femininity and my Christian identity, at the expense of my university identity, helped balance the power dynamics considerably. When I left both Lebanon and Egypt, there were families of converts who texted me on my mobile to make sure I arrived safely back in the United Kingdom. Families often invited me to meals and told me that they would take care of me like their sister or daughter. In Egypt, this dynamic was further enhanced by the fact that my parents accompanied me on the first ten days of my trip. Many people who became important informants met me as a "girl", the daughter of my father, as opposed to a university researcher in my own right.

Cindi Katz wrote of similar dynamics when she first arrived for her fieldwork in Sudan, whereby the villagers with whom she interacted, treated her as merely a friend of a government-appointed educator who was living in the same village at the same time (Katz 1994:68-69). There was a sense in which her importance was undermined, arguably decreasing her perceived power position, but this ultimately did not inhibit her work. In fact, though frustrated, she admitted that it may have facilitated her research. I felt a similar dynamic in my fieldwork and believe that it helped balance the power dynamics significantly. In addition, in keeping with feminist theory, I enjoyed a certain added rapport with other women, and I believe that had I been a man, developing a connection would have been more difficult with almost all participants, female and male, due to man's culturally dominant position. Nonetheless, it was important that I recognise that the participants in this study could automatically assume I was approaching them from a position of dominance. The greatest degree of acceptance I could hope for was to be seen as a sympathiser, as "wise".

I also had to be sensitive to the implications of an in-group favouritism that I witnessed among members of MBB communities. This favouritism naturally implied a negative bias against outsiders. Though I was generally warmly welcomed into their circles, it was clear to me that I was nonetheless somewhat of an intruder. The presence of an intruder could intensify an uncritical attitude that they already held toward others more "like them". Furthermore, I had to be careful not to get involved in cliques. Though almost all converts shared a common definition of who was an insider, this did not mean that they accepted all insiders equally. Their strongest in-group bias was often reserved specifically for the group of friends with whom they had regular contact, or who they considered to be a part of their fellowship group. Sometimes participants would question my desire to meet with people from other groups, apparently assuming that they and their friends were sufficiently representative.

In fact, there was a general suspicion of unknown and untrusted people, and a number of participants were actually more willing to trust me, as a foreigner, than any other fellow Arab, including other people "like them". A few of the people I met made it very clear that they avoid unnecessary contact with other Arabs. On the other hand, one woman complained that in her MBB community, introduction to foreigners was a statement of status within their group, that "average" group members were unlikely to have the opportunity to meet someone like me. Therefore, in order to gain the deepest and broadest access, as an outsider, it was crucial that I gain the trust of insiders, but that I not participate in their relational structure, particularly that I try to avoid contributing to existing divisions and identifiers of status. It was important to stay an outsider, albeit a trusted outsider.

Finally, I had to be constantly reflecting on how my actions might affect the people I was researching (Jacobsen and Landau 2003:192). I was aware that my presence in the field had the potential to affect the lives of converts because they are especially volatile. Since the majority of citizens of the Arab world are Muslim, converts feel like a threatened minority in their societies, and usually choose to keep their conversion hidden from all but a few trusted people. After all, conversion carries with it a stigma as significant as, if not stronger than, sexual or criminal deviance. This research was highly sensitive, conducted in an underground community: besides the normal ethical demands of maintaining people's confidence in research, I needed to be particularly sensitive to the ways in which the participants wanted their identities protected. I was aware that if certain stakeholders knew about the purpose of my research and also knew who I was meeting with, I had already put my contacts at risk. The specific sensitivities varied from one individual to another, but I needed to adhere to a high level of caution and I tried to be highly sensitive to their fears, especially when seeking access. This was one of the main reasons that I limited the length of my stay in the field. Some participants encouraged me in pointing out that my determination to dress in a culturally respectable way, speak Arabic, and follow other cultural expectations for a young woman, made their association with me somewhat less problematic, but even so, the times spent negotiating these concerns were those when I most acutely felt my "outsider" status.

Reflexivity continued well beyond my field research days, as I re-read the narratives I had collected and analysed them. I approached the analysis as a dialogue between myself, the researcher, and the researched community. To the extent possible, albeit to a lesser extent once I left the field, I involved members of the researched community in the process of analysis. This is in keeping with Ruthellen Josselson's suggestion that research be conducted with the purpose of distilling, elucidating and illuminating the process of analysis, involving a good deal of dialogue with the researched and careful reflexivity on the part of the researcher.

One of my primary gatekeepers was a convert who had lived outside his home in the Arab world for many years; he sometimes called himself schizophrenic because he would frequently and quickly switch between different cultures and different ways of perceiving a situation. One of the greatest compliments he paid to me was that he considered me to be like him: just as confused, since I had grown up in a multicultural environment and adopted yet new cultures in adulthood. This study presents an analysis of converts in the Arab world through the eyes of a social researcher, and in my case a researcher who sees herself as as outsider not only to the community she is researching but also to the communities to which she may be ascribed as belonging. I approached the analysis from this perspective. I cannot claim that this made the quality of my analysis better, or more "pure". Nor would I suggest that it throws the validity of the analysis into question, merely that when reading my analysis, this is the reflexive position from which I have written it.

Ultimately, this book presents my telling of the story of converts from Islam to a Christian faith throughout the Arab world, which is why it is important to be aware of my identity and my position in the research. As a young female Christian, I do believe I am uniquely placed to analyse this topic. As I worked through the analysis of the data, I had a sense that I was approaching it not from the uncritical eye of an insider, nor from the unsympathetic eye of an outsider. I am not solely a British academician, nor an American Christian, nor a cultural Brazilian, nor a scholar who lived several years in the Middle East. I am all of those things and none of those things. When analysing the data, I similarly tried to look at it from all of these perspectives, from none of them, and even from an insider perspective as best I could. The portrait presented in the coming chapters, therefore, reflects that unusual combination.

Cooperative Advocacy

I was working on this project with a community that had no interest in being treated as the "other". Their frequent reminders that I was an outsider, were partly an expression of autonomy. Indeed, it is not my intention for this project to contribute to the heritage of Westerners discussing exotic indigenous communities amongst themselves, using Western paradigms.

Researching a community of religious people who have converted out of the dominant religion in their society, into a globally dominant religion, brings with it a unique twist of roles. Religious establishment, particularly Christianity, has often been a powerful institution in society, and the sociological tradition has been to support the rights of minority religious groups and non-religious people in their struggle against the dominance of religious Christians. This study follows in that tradition, except in this case the minority religious group is the group that has chosen a faith which has a long history of dominance, in a context where they are not afforded the right to do so. Most converts I met were eager to stand up for their rights and see those defended against the powerful institutions, simultaneously well-aware that they could easily be objectified by Westerners who treat them as not always knowing what is best for themselves. This complaint was most often lodged against Christian missionaries in the interviews I conducted, but the converts I met were determined to assert their autonomy, not only to Western institutions, but also against Islam, the majority religion in their own countries.

Feminist methodology provided a helpful framework for forming a research project around these concerns. This research can support the needs of converts in a way that feminist research is used to support the needs of women, under the umbrella of advocacy research. The literature on feminist research helps to explain that this is not a flaw in the methodology: this relationship to my research is not only valid but is essential when the researched community feels voiceless, and it can be beneficial to the quality of information produced (Arvanitakis 2012:101). The idea of "value free" research has been seriously questioned, especially by the Frankfurt school, and is now generally understood to be an unattainable goal. Feminist researchers often argue that not only is it impossible to separate research from a cause that it might serve, but better data often results when one embraces the fullness of the cause of the group being studied. There is an argument that better theories will result when one is participating in the dynamics of a movement instead of simply being a distant spectator. So my goal is to connect and identify with the subjects of my research, but only insofar as I maintain a degree of objectivity.

Before I began my field research, the converts whom I had already met had made very clear to me their determination not to be undermined by outsiders, and so I adopted the attitude that Nigel Fielding called "coproducing fieldwork" (Fielding 1993:150), or Himika Bhattacharya referred to as "critical collaborative ethnography" (Bhattacharya 2008:305). The research subjects were actually interpretive actors who worked through the data, jointly drawing conclusions and by so doing contributing to social action and social change. It is important to state that this is not the same thing as maintaining a naturalistic indiscriminate attitude toward the researched, it simply means that I involved them both in my determination of what needed to be studied and in analysis of the data. Considering not only the power dynamics underlining this study, but also that this explores the way individuals approach their own identities and develop their communities, it seemed only right to focus on issues that they believe are important and to involve them in understanding those issues. In my commitment to support the cause of improving the plight of converts from a Muslim background to a Christian faith. I felt and still feel strongly that my primary obligation is to those who I am studying. I recognise that this is rather idealistic of me, and feel I have only somewhat succeeded, but I believe it is the right goal to which to have aspired.

While sympathy was important in the field, it was also important for me to maintain a healthy degree of scepticism (Alexander 2000:27-28). In some research there is a tendency whereby too much trust is afforded the subjects, sacrificing the rigour of the research methodology for the sake of a sense of covenant with the researched community. Research with victimised or stigmatised groups is sometimes particularly susceptible to a relaxing of standards for research rigour, out of sympathy or advocacy for the researched group, but "data that are scientifically and ethically collected create a powerful tool for policymakers, and better methods will enable... productive and critical debates with the social sciences, which have so far remained at a remove from the field" (Jacobsen and Landau 2003:201). In other words, the research will mean little and bear little weight if it is not held up to the highest of standards.

Taking insider concerns into account, while maintaining the expected academic rigours, should result in excellent research, but sometimes it can feel more like trying not to fall off of a tightrope. I found it helpful to keep in mind that maintaining rigorous research does not mean developing an inflexible research schedule: it means being willing to ask all the questions that may emerge. In fact, ethnographic and narrative research are not meant to be tightly pre-defined: in a fieldwork setting the researcher has minimal control over the research setting or the interaction that will entail, and the communication between researcher and researched must be two-way (Cassell 1980:29-30). Being open in the process of deciding what is relevant data and how to use it is fundamental to ethnographic research, and the discovery process is an integral part of the research (Mattingly 2005:460). I focus on narratives in my fieldwork research because they help provide a fuller picture of the values and lifestyles of the participants, their motivations and risks, and their response under stress. This approach proved very effective, and so much sociologically valid data became available simply through asking participants to tell me their stories.

However, co-producing fieldwork should go beyond data. Participants are exactly that: participants in the research project. They gave valuable analytical insight, suggestions, and connections to other converts and other researchers. They not only supported my research, but also my role as a researcher. They did not generally try to influence the sources of my data, and on the few occasions they did, they respected my request that they avoid allowing personal inclinations to get in the way of the data collection. Advocacy research should always include a component of actively involving the researched as active participants and not just as a means to an end.

Relationship with the Field

The close bonds that this type of research entails, have encouraged me to be acutely reflexive about my relationship with participants. Bonds of friendship are a natural component of any ethnographic fieldwork, and the ease of communication in this age of globalisation has made boundaries between fieldwork and the rest of life much more difficult to define. There has been a constant tension between my relationship to participants as stranger, as interviewer and as friend. Not only my identity as researcher was at stake: so was the validity of the research. Sometimes, when interacting with people who have stories full of pain, abuse, and conflicted relationships, it is difficult to hear them with sympathy but also with objectivity. But to do justice to their accounts, the researcher must try (Jacobsen and Landau 2003:185).

While some may argue that a clear distance from the field may guarantee more methodologically dependable, less messy data, such an approach is reminiscent of an era when the anthropologist left the field never to return. "The time is probably past when a fieldworker left the field, never to be seen again by his people. With better means of transportation, and with growing interest in restudy, many an anthropologist plays with the idea of going back some day, and occasionally one actually returns" (Kloos 1969:511). Today, nearly four decades after Kloos wrote that, I can easily maintain contact with participants via mobile phone and various forms of Internet communication. Over the years since I left the field, most of these relationships have faded, but I do still interact with some of them from time to time. They have become, at the very least, acquaintances for life. I can and do return to "the field".

Actually, from the beginning I had no such expectation that I would thoroughly distance myself from the field, since I had lived in the Middle East for three years previously and, in fact, reentering Lebanon to begin my field research was more like a homecoming from the year I spent in England, a country previously unknown to me, than it was an arrival in an exotic "field". Many of my research participants and gatekeepers were good friends from the time that I had lived there. While I have been learning to compartmentalise those relationships and interactions in the course of the research process, I cannot say that by leaving the field I have left the field behind. In Egypt, though I had no previous relationships, I made friendships that lasted well beyond my departure at the end of my field research there.

In a sense, we are always already in the field and we never leave the field (Katz 1994:67). To be sure, indigenous and feminist researchers by definition take issue with the assumption of many classic anthropologists that distance from the field is essential to good research, but there is an important distinction between complete distance and compartmentalisation of one's role as a researcher among the researched (Gaston and Zweerink 2004:194-195). When an individual moves to a new context and learns that context as well as s/he can, s/he cannot hope to come "home" unchanged. Our field of study becomes our lives, and any distinct breaking off from the field is rarely more than an unrealistic expectation.

Some ethnographers argue that it would actually be unethical to force a distance into relationships created through fieldwork. Cheryl Mattingly critiques the impact of research boards' expectations of "academic distance" from her participants, stating that "attempts to ensure privacy can sometimes seem more like rendering someone anonymous than protecting them... as though I were treating her just like any other 'research subject'" (Mattingly 2005:456). She goes on to ask how the silence and distance which are often considered professional conduct can be ethical, because they do not honour the very significant investment that the people being researched have made in the relationship. The researcher gets data, and perhaps a degree or a publication or respect; what do the researched get?

Many fieldworkers have stories of difficult situations where participants had unreal expectations of their relationship with the researcher, or where people discovered that things they had told the researcher in confidence became data.[1] Though we are sure to obtain informed consent and regularly remind the people we are researching that we are conducting field research, and that they are contributors to the process, such messy situations are sure to arise. The conclusion is that, while it would be unethical to become friends with someone merely for the sake of data, friendship is not easy to avoid, nor should it be avoided, and how it is managed must be to some extent field-specific (Benson and Thomas 2010:680).

In my relationship with the field, I felt little expectation from the participants, except that I treat them as they treated me: like fellow brothers and sisters in Christ. They had, too often, felt like they were not treated as such by other co-religionists and they had told me of their hurt. Many participants told me that they felt like foreigners come and meet with them, take their picture or do a Bible study with them, and then leave; the participants felt like they were simply being "ticked off a list". I did not want to contribute to this sense of abandonment, nor do I believe it would have been ethical to do so (Renzetti and Lee 1993:101). Though most of the participants in this project had not experienced being the researched before, they had experienced being the "target" of foreign Christians, and I believe it would be wrong to leave them once again hurt by neglect, this time at the hand of a foreign researcher. While few friendships have lasted the test of time, I tried to stay in touch with as many of the participants as I could for as long as it was natural after I left the field – treating them as the friends they had indeed become.

Reciprocity was crucial: the interviewer giving a little of herself in the exchange, opening herself up to the same emotional vulnerability that she is asking of the researched (Edwards 1993:192-193). Truly, many converts who I met did not have many close relationships, and they had shared so openly, in a sense given me a part of themselves. So there was usually a distinct change in how people interacted with me after the interview, relative to before the interview, and that defined the place of each unique interview in the larger scope of my field research time. Each interview seemed to result in a new or altered relationship, in part because of the intimacy of what they shared with me. In one case, the participant was a prior friend of mine, and the fact that he was sharing intimate details with me seemed to have such an effect on our friendship that it took some months before our interaction seemed normal again.

It bears mention that I felt some discomfort in most of my interviews with men. Originally, I had planned to conduct all interviews with men with either their wives or a male friend of mine present, but circumstances made that difficult to achieve in some cases, and in fact many participants and

---

[1] Appell's 1978 book of fieldwork case studies contains a sample of such stories.

gatekeepers had the expectation that a professional single woman would interview a man in relative privacy. I do not think that this interfered with the data, merely that it caused some strain on the conversation, especially in discussions about their relationships with women, and particularly single men's thoughts about marriage. With most of these individuals, I actually did not pursue any contact after the formal interview because I did not want to give the wrong impression (especially considering that many of them had told me that they would be interested in marrying a foreign woman).

However, with most of the rest of the participants, it seemed that it was appropriate to pursue a social relationship after the interview. I managed at least one follow-up visit with most women and couples who I met, and with some a genuine friendship was established or was deepened. Besides the fact that they seemed to feel a special connection with someone who had heard many of their intimate experiences and thoughts, one theme that emerged from the interviews was a deep desire for community. Several told me that they were looking for genuine friendships to fill the hole created as a result of no longer connecting intimately with Muslim friends and family. Since they shared openly with me, a deep level of trust developed quickly, and I felt an obligation to respond in some way to their need for relationship even though I could not actually provide the deep family connection that they were looking for.

Ultimately, I had to be both researcher and friend. This brought up another ethical dilemma. All the participants knew that I was conducting research, and that anything they told me could be used as data for the research project. I tried to explain this to them as clearly as possible, and make sure that my research came up from time to time in our conversations so as to remind them. Even so, I wonder if some of them really *knew* that our relationship was not just a friendship, that it was also data. Methodology textbooks and ethical statements emphasise the importance of informed consent, stating that research respondents sometimes need to be reminded regularly that they are participating in a research project, because just claiming to have told them once is not enough (Librett and Perrone 2010). Similar to Benson and Thomas's description of their ethnographic research with tobacco farmers (Benson and Thomas 2010), I found that I could and should endeavour at all times to achieve this, but when juggling relationships and research, that is not always an easy mandate. I worked hard to ensure ongoing informed consent, but I have no guarantees that I succeeded.

I often felt like I was standing on an ethical boundary when I invested in friendship with participants. For the many reasons listed above, I believe it was the correct, and most ethical, thing to do, but it is impossible for a field researcher to not be observing a research-related context in which she finds herself. So it was natural that I obtained data out of those friendships. The strong support for this project that I received from many converts, and from the participants in this study, the fact that they made it clear to me that they think this is an important topic of research, is my justification for using conversations out of friendship, for data. I believe that the individuals involved value what we are studying enough to see their relationship with me put to this use.

Analysis and Critique

The delicate relationship with my research participants does raise concerns about the final product and how different groups might use it. I became friends with many of the participants, and there is a natural preoccupation with how this could affect our relationship and what constitutes appropriate use of the trust they put in me. Certainly, many participants shared more openly with me because they expected me to use what they told me in a way that they would see as beneficial for their own purposes. My ethical considerations with regards to the research extend beyond the fieldwork to the means by which I share my findings with others: while doing justice to the knowledge obtained, it is also important to continue to treat those who informed the study with respect in the ways by which, and the venues in which, I describe them (Librett and Perrone 2010:741, Livholts 2012:3).

Janet Finch wrote of a similar concern in her compelling article, "It's Great to Have Someone to Talk to: Ethics and Politics of Interviewing Women". Just like I found with converts, she found that when interviewing women in a personal way, as a fellow woman with shared experiences, her participants were almost too willing to share openly and unreservedly with her (Finch 1993:168). Similar to Finch's experience, I recall that one participant told me before the interview, "I am happy to tell my story because the testimony of others has been a real encouragement to me, so maybe through my testimony I can encourage others," but at the end of the interview, she thanked me for the opportunity, saying, "Talking about my testimony has helped me remember how God has acted in my life over the years."

Finch observed that in an open-ended conversational interview of this sort, in which participants feel particularly comfortable sharing openly, the researcher finds herself in a place of moral obligation to her participants, because it is possible to unintentionally betray the women's trust. "I mean, rather, 'betrayal' in an indirect and collective sense, that is, undermining the interests of women in general by my use of the material given to me by my interviewees. It is betrayal none the less, because the basis upon which the information has been given is the trust placed in one woman by another" (Finch 1993:177). In my situation, the dynamic was based on the trust placed in one "believer" by another.

Therefore, Finch makes an important point about the sensitivity surrounding using the accounts of the researched in a way that honours them and does not take advantage of them (Finch 1993:178). She cites an argument that many make, which is that the main benefit of any research is the growth of the body of sociological knowledge, but I agree with her in her conclusion that that is not enough, that knowledge is only valuable if it is put to good use. This approach is honest, but it presented challenges when my findings were not always what the researched wanted them to be. Again, I find myself on this tight-rope that I have created for myself through this research, trying to treat the data with academic integrity without abusing in any way the trust which was granted me in obtaining this data.

It has been useful to me to remember that helping the MBB community may involve raising questions of critical analysis, hopefully with the added analytic perspective of a researcher in my unique reflexive position. For me, this was particularly challenging as I tried to represent the reality of all Muslim-background converts to a Christian faith as a whole, but also the different approaches and factions within that larger community. I imagine that some individuals may feel betrayed when they realise that my conclusions about certain issues do not fully fall in line with their personal views.

While looking to understand carefully the narratives and to find deeper themes, approaching the texts critically but without too much suspicion, I had to be aware of the limitations of my data. The writing of a narrative fixes it in time: it is not only limited by who said it (the interviewee) and who transcribed it (the researcher), but also by the fact that it is a snapshot of an individual's perspective at one particular point in time. Stories are, in a sense, windows into a specific moment of a specific world, which present not just people's experiences but also how they perceive those experiences at the time of telling (Gubrium and Holstein 2008:244-245).

Since my field research ended, I have learned that at least one participant has returned to Islam, and some of her Christian friends suspect that she was in fact only pretending to have converted in the first place. Another participant has not returned to Islam, but he has also not hidden the fact that he may have lost interest in his adopted faith. After hearing this and looking back at their narratives, I came to the conclusion that this could potentially change my entire analysis, but that I could not be sure in which way. I found no evidence from our conversations which led me to doubt that they had been mostly earnest in what they shared with me at the time that they shared it with me: this was simply new information that emerged with the passage of time. Their stories likely do not reflect the entire truth at the time of telling, and certainly do not reflect the truth of today, but they still provide insight into how they thought through the issues we discussed. I could have attempted to add more of myself to the data by reinterpreting their narratives, but as art critic Susan Sontag wrote, over-interpretation can quickly lead to alteration of the entire text (Sontag 1966). Instead, I prefer to acknowledge that my analysis is incomplete and hope that future research will add to the understanding of this community and explore more in-depth other layers of their experience. The contribution of this study is an in-depth understanding of how the converts I met approached their lives as converts at the time that I met them, and how they expressed their conceptualisation of their lives.

Tawhid: Perfect Unity

Over and over, when in the field, I was reminded how closely intertwined Islamic doctrine is, both with people's sense of their own identity and with how community life is structured in Arab Muslim communities. Community life is largely built around religious traditions, and practices are readily accredited to *sunna* or Qur'an. This strong undercurrent of religious doctrine informs much of life, and remains with people raised in Muslim families for the rest of their lives, so Islamic doctrine provides a useful framework for understanding how many people from a Muslim background approach their new lives as converts to a new faith system.

Islamic doctrine has been used extensively by missiologists to consider how to frame the Gospel and Christianity in a way that makes sense to Muslims around the world. For example, Fouad Accad, a prominent Lebanese Christian pastor, used references from both the Bible and the Qur'an that mutually support his doctrinal points, claiming, "No sincere, clear-thinking Muslim can deny what the Qur'an affirms about Christ's divine characteristics." (Accad 1997:113). In keeping with this position, missiological groups developed approaches such as the popular "Camel Method" for evangelisation, a tool which is used by Christians to explain their beliefs to their Muslim friends using Islamic scripture. A number of Christian groups have adopted the practice of explaining the Christian Gospel using Muslim references and terminology.

The relevance of Islamic doctrine to sociological study of Arab Muslim communities is also well-established. Moroccan sociologist Fatima Mernissi famously developed the concept of the *hijab* which, she argued, was introduced as an essential religious concept in the *Qur'an* but has much more widespread and important purposes than the seclusion of women. History intersected with doctrine to transform the importance of the *hijab*, with far-reaching consequences on the roles and rights afforded to women in communities that adhere to those doctrines (Mernissi 1991a:190-191). This one example from Mernissi's sociology reflects a conceptualisation of values that can be seen repeatedly, at various levels of society. In many communities of the Arab world, individuals make decisions on the basis of communal values that are rooted in a set of beliefs attributed to Islam. Muslim theology, doctrine and history must be taken as foundational when developing a sociological formulation for understanding a Muslim context (Asad 2003:85-86).

To provide insight into the dreams and ideals many converts grew up with, I will explore two fundamental Islamic doctrines and their implications for converts' experience of life adhering to a new faith. In this chapter, I will discuss the concept of *tawhid*, which means, simply, unity. The next chapter will explore the implications of *umma*, that is, the doctrine surrounding the importance of community.

Doctrine and History of Tawhid

Islam is a religion defined by unity. Unity in the oneness, or *tawhid*, of God. Unity in life between lifestyle and faith. Unity in society between politics and religion. Unity in the community defined by conformity. This is based primarily on the doctrinal importance of the unity of God, in a religion whose creed begins with the affirmation that "there is no God but the one God". *Tawhid* has been used by various different scholars to explain a great deal in Muslim societies: after all, unity is emphasised in many different ways and in many different contexts by adherents to Islam. It is a rediscovering of "the primordial bond between God and humanity" (Zaidi 2011:64)

In the shared history of the early years of Islam, the focus of Muhammad's mission was to teach the Arabs to live lives in submission to only one god – the Only One God. Before Muhammad[1] started receiving his revelations which were to become the Qur'an, the Meccan community, and in particular Muhammad's tribe of Quraysh, was increasingly individualistic. Loyalty to individual gods was on the rise and becoming a source of tension. Therefore, Muhammad's chief endeavour may have been to point people in the direction of the One God as a means of restoring peace and unity to Mecca.

According to Mernissi, when Muhammad returned to Mecca as a successful religious leader, "the truce was between the Meccans and Allah, with the Meccans renouncing *shirk*, the freedom to think and choose their religion, which was incarnated by the 360 gods enthroned in the Ka'ba. In exchange Allah guaranteed peace in the city, where violence was a problem" (Mernissi 2002:85). The most important thing for a Muslim to learn was that God was one and did not share (the root meaning of the word *shirk*) the godhead with any other. Once a believer was convicted of the oneness and transcendence of God, s/he was expected to conform to the behaviour commanded by God and his messenger. *Tawhid* extends from an understanding of the unity of God to unity in all areas of life. Mernissi writes, "Opposition to the One would forever have a negative color, and the words that express it today – words like *hizb* (party) and *shi'a* (group with a different opinion), which are rooted in [the early years of Muhammad's prophetic career] – have a sectarian character" (Mernissi 2002:99).

---

[1] Since most of the participants in this study have rejected the Prophethood of Muhammad, I will refer to him by name, but wish here to acknowledge the respected title to which he is generally referred, that of Prophet Peace Be Upon Him.

This emphasis on oneness has given rise to a remarkable cohesiveness of history, tradition and practices among Muslims. The importance of Islamic doctrine, particularly the emphasis on unity in theology as well as in everyday life, is rooted in a well-known shared history. History is important to every people, and many Arab Muslims place especially great value on history. Middle East historian Bernard Lewis has argued repeatedly that history has played a more important role in Muslim societies than elsewhere during the past century: "This acute awareness of the past, even a distant past, is a characteristic feature of Islamic society and is in marked contrast with the growing disregard by Westerners of their own past" (Lewis and Churchill 2009:72). Indeed, the early years of Muslim history are remarkably well-documented.

The stories from the early years of Islam comprise a set of "narratives" which have given rise to coherent themes by which many Muslims all around the world define values, practices and a sense of Muslim unity (Halverson et. al. 2011). Stories from the history of Islam are told frequently in popular discourse and provide individuals with a sense of connectivity to the worldwide community of Islam. These narratives have helped Muslims around the world to develop a stronger understanding of common causes and enemies, shared identity, and vision for the future. While such a perspective is criticised by many scholars as reductionist, because different groups can tell different stories and interpret them in different ways, this idea of a shared identity rooted in a common historical narrative resonates with my experience and with that of other scholars who have spent time in Arab Muslim communities. Many stories are frequently repeated in various different circles across the Middle East, creating a shared understanding of religion and reality.[2]

Most particularly for this discussion, the stories of the life of the Muslim prophet Muhammad have been carefully recorded and studied, and many Muslims see in his life important insights into the nature of the religious experience (Armstrong 2006:14). The example of his life has been taken as a paradigm for Muslim practice ever since. One participant explained to me that a "normal" Muslim can be distinguished from a "secular" Muslim by the fact that s/he follows the example of the Prophet as he was and how he lived his life, and that s/he loves him. In fact, many participants continued to speak highly of Muhammad and emphasised to me that it is important that they show respect to him and to the stories of his life when conversing with Muslims, regardless of what they personally have come to believe about him.

There are various documented connections between incidents in Muhammad's life and specific Muslim traditions (Armstrong 2002:51). One of the most respected Muslim theologians of all time, Imam al-Ghazali (d. 1111), instructed the faithful to follow the *sunna* (sayings and actions of the Prophet Muhammad), in as much detail as possible, including Muhammad's habits,

[2] See Halverson et. al. 2011 for a more thorough discussion of this topic.

style of eating, how he slept and how he talked. Doing so, he said, was the key to happiness and fulfilment, and these traditions have become means by which Muslim identity has become distinct. Islamic law (*shari'a*) developed out of this constructed common Muslim history, which is largely based on the *sunna*, the sayings and practices of the prophet Muhammad. Arguably most Muslims, even many non-practising Muslims, still adhere to it, at least in part. It includes a well-developed family law, which contains rules referring to such things as a wife's behaviour, her duties to her husband and vice-versa, and rules about adoption. There is also a strong set of traditions and rituals which are traced to the *sunna*, in keeping with Muslim doctrine. These shared traditions strengthen the sense of unity among Muslims, which in turn provides a strong basis for structuring individual and community values around the doctrinal principle of unity.

Today, 1400 years after the life of the prophet Muhammad, *tawhid* continues to buttress a sense of common history and values among Muslims from diverse backgrounds, worldwide. Muslim-majority countries can be found across much of the globe, and there are Muslim minorities spread throughout the rest of the world. Many adherents to Islam, especially the diverse communities of Muslims in the Arab world, do have more in common than a simple creed, and are often very proud of these commonalities (Zubaida 2009).

Even though global Islam is relatively cohesive considering its size and breadth, in reality there are multiple interpretations and expressions of Islam. Nonetheless, these variations are often dismissed or downgraded in importance, and Muslim communities often choose not to acknowledge the existing diversity in understandings of Islam, instead promoting an idea of "pure" Islam (Zubaida 2011). A sense of a cohesive Muslim identity is important to many Muslims, but that is becoming contentious in immigrant communities and in contexts influenced by globalisation, where the myth of unity in the worldwide community of Muslims is being questioned (Lewis 2007). So we find that for many Muslims, there is a sense of worldwide Muslim unity and cohesiveness, but it is a retrospectively constructed identity (Gaudeul 1999:59, Roald 2006:53-55). There is, in fact, no epicentre in Islam or single authority defining what it means to be "Muslim". There are movements underway to build solidarity and a transnational rhetoric of Islam, but so far those efforts have borne little fruit (Makris 2007:54-55).

In the Arab world, a fair bit of rhetoric has promoted the idea that to be Arab is to be Muslim. Michel Aflaq, a Syrian Christian who helped found the nationalistic Ba'ath party, described Islam as the culture of the Arabs (Zubaida 2011:179). While this idea was not particularly well-received by Muslim political reformers, the idea that Islam is integrated into Arab culture has remained strong in countries of the Middle East, including Lebanon and Egypt where the bulk of this research took place. Muslim political movements have emphasised an inherent compatibility between being 'Arab' and being 'Muslim'. Over the course of the twentieth century, which was marked by a number of Arab nationalist movements, Muslim political reformers increasingly encouraged the Muslim communities in their countries to identify with Islam as a way of life, rather than with Arab culture (Zubaida 2011:180-181). This rhetoric may have further reinforced a sense of *tawhid* in how many Muslims, especially Arab Muslims, perceive their identity.

Tawhid of Life

Tawhid in life may be described as a behaviour and an attitude which reveal and illustrate the *tawhid* in God. A believer in Islam may be defined first and foremost by adherence to a creed, but this will likely find its expression in how the believer lives his/her life, demonstrating his/her *islam* (submission) in living out an integrated Muslim life free of distractions from commitment to God alone (Armstrong 2006:74).

Islam is, for many of the devout, lived through practices. From the very beginning of Muslim history, the rituals of Islam were very carefully set out. These included prayer times, fasting times, marriage laws, and child rearing. All of this may then become a form of devotion to God, through the Qur'an, God's uncreated word. Reverence for the Qur'an, in particular, is a form of reverence for God, and is considered by many to be fundamental for living a unified life.

Many Arab Muslims I have met approach their religion as a collection of highly organised and procedural practices which are attributed to Islam. Everyday acts such as housecleaning and bathing are often given a distinct religious meaning. For example, in an Arab Muslim household where I lived for some time, I was given strict instructions about which shoes to wear in each part of the house, what types of personal hygiene activities I should conduct where, and at which specific moments I was to give my roommate privacy. Each of these instructions was explained to me with a doctrinal justification, or with a statement attributed to the Prophet.

In the early years of Islam, there was a debate regarding the role of such unquestioning piety, but devotion to the Qur'an as well as to the Prophet Muhammad became the dominant thinking as Sunni Islam developed and became the largest most potent thread of the religion. The roots of Islam were also emphasised, especially the reported and recorded sayings and practices of the Prophet Muhammad. Reverence for the Qur'an and the Prophet Muhammad became the means by which Islam was kept unified around a set of clearly defined early principles (Armstrong 2002:49). Mystical worshippers of God are called "Sufis". They started out as a parallel Muslim movement but most devoted Muslims now have some Sufi characteristics, expressed through the devotion that they integrate into all areas of life.

Imam Al-Ghazali was himself a Sufi Muslim, having dedicated his later life to an experiential knowledge of God. He had a mystical belief in God, but he also believed that one could experience and know God through following the directives of Islamic law. In his "The Beginning of Guidance", he quoted the Prophet as giving the following word from God: "Nothing brings men near to me like the performance of what I made obligatory for them" (in Watt 1995:100). He proceeded to instruct the faithful as to how to live their lives, including how to sleep, wake, eat, pray, and pass the hours of the day. Even the intricacies of relieving oneself were instructed as a religious activity. It is also through physical acts that sin is committed. Al-Ghazali wrote, "You disobey or sin against God only through the parts of your body" (in Watt 1995:145), and proceeded to explain in detail how to avoid sinning through different activities involving specific body parts. Even Muslims who are largely secular in their beliefs and lifestyle may have a relatively high level of participation in Muslim rituals, both because of the strongly ingrained nature of Muslim values in their upbringing (i.e. not eating pork), and for the sake of family cohesiveness and communal continuity (i.e. fasting during Ramadan as a family event).[3]

Over the course of history, and as a result of various perceived political and cultural threats to the *umma* (the Muslim community), Muslim tradition, particularly among the Sunni majority of the Middle East, has become more set in its rituals. A large number of Muslim clerics and political leaders have tended to avoid debate, preferring a dogged unity of opinion about religious issues, claiming that "the gates of *ijtihad* [independent reasoning] are closed", although it bears mention that this trend has been reversing in intellectual circles during recent decades (Lewis and Churchill 2009:29, Brown 2010). As a result, Middle Eastern Muslim communities continue to rely on the traditions passed down from the days of Muhammad in a way not very different from the practices of their forbears. This has confirmed the close relationship between belief and ritual, with belief expressed through ritual. For many, belief has become defined even more by Muslim practices than by the Muslim creed.

Tawhid of Society

Religion is not only one with the details of an individual or family's lifestyle: it is also one with governance in what is considered by many Muslim clerics and political leaders to be the ideal Muslim society. Historically, this can be traced to roots in Muhammad's lifetime. Muhammad was the leader of a community, starting with the first Muslims when they emigrated from Mecca to Medina. Through wars, conquests, and treaties, he became the leader of most of Arabia before he died (Armstrong 2006:204-205). Today, many Muslims think of the golden age of Islam as the years when the religious Muslim world was a polity, especially in the early years of conquest following Muhammad's death. Unity bolsters Islam's claim to universality.

The foundations of Islam included a political mandate, seen by many Muslims as unique to Islam. Muslim scholar Ibn Khaldun (d. 1406), upheld by

---

[3] See Lazar et al 2002 for a description of a similar tendency among non-religious Jews.

many contemporary Muslim academics as one of the greatest historians and social analysts of Islam, but dismissed by some Western scholars because he wrote from the perspective of a Muslim believer (Ahmed 2003:76-77, Zaidi 2011:14),[4] wrote, "In the Muslim community, the holy war is a religious duty, because of the universalism of the Muslim mission and (the obligation to) convert everybody to Islam either by persuasion or by force. Therefore, the caliphate and royal authority are united in Islam, so that the person in charge can devote the available strength to both of them at the same time" (Khaldun 1967:183).

According to Khaldun's analysis of religion in the fourteenth century, because other religious groups did not have a universal mission, the religious leaders in those other groups were not expected to be concerned with power politics at all. They did not have the religious duty of *jihad*, which may be translated in this text as "holy war." In other contexts the concept of *jihad*, considered by most Muslim theologians to be a fundamental religious duty, is translated more simply as "struggle", and is most commonly interpreted to mean the internal spiritual struggle faced by a devout Muslim. For Khaldun, however, *jihad* refers to a battle that is a part of the universalising mission of Islam. Khaldun's position was that political and religious authority may overlap in other religions, but this is mostly due to a strong sense of what he calls *asabiyya*, or "group feeling": a strong loyalty to one's group. It is not because "they are under obligation to gain power over other nations, as is the case with Islam" (Khaldun 1967:183).

Many Muslims still understand their reality in this framework. Because of this unity between religion and politics in Islam, many political leaders of Muslim-majority nations have closely identified their role in politics with their attitude toward religion. This can be particularly well illustrated by the approach taken by Muslim modernisers, who have generally also been secularisers. Mustafa Kemal Ataturk is a particularly notable example of this: as he endeavoured to bring modernity to Turkey, he suppressed the Muslim religion in both the public and private spheres. Even though or, more accurately, because the Turkish government is considered secular, it has also

---

[4] Ali Zaidi makes an interesting argument about Ibn Khaldun's writing, suggesting that it has been grossly misinterpreted by two opposing camps of scholars: on one hand, the so-called "Orientalists" have upheld Khaldun as a dispassionate social scientist of the world he lived in; on the other hand, more recent critical scholarship have expressed concerns that his work is far from dispassionate and bear no comparison to social science at all. In fact, Zaidi suggests, Ibn Khaldun took a rare and unique perspective, one which shamelessly integrated personal faith and belief into a thoughtful analysis of society where he lived. His work is not merely empirical, since faith plays a key role, and yet it is an honest assessment of his social milieu. This is noteworthy in a sociological study about faith because, by necessity, this research must take a similar perspective: acknowledging converts' experience of faith as something that is real while still analysing the results of their faith decision as objectively as possible.

played an active role in regulating religion (Shankland 1999, Ameli 2002:105).[5]

In recent years, the Turkish government's interest in suppressing or promoting religion has weakened, and there is movement in various other Muslim nations toward greater separation between politics and religion. The application of such values is therefore increasingly variable. It remains, however, that the perception that politics and society are inherently religious concerns, is shared by many if not most Muslims, arguably even more fervently in local traditional communities than on the intellectual plane of geopolitics. This is why the idea of *tawhid* in society is of sociological importance for understanding the paradigm from which many Arab MBBs come.

Converts and Tawhid

Because of the importance of *tawhid* in many Muslim communities, converts from Islam to a Christian faith often come from a background where unity of faith, duties and society is an underlying feature of everyday life, and is doctrinally justified. This value system may complicate the process of adjustment to a new Christian life, especially considering that many join streams of Christianity which encourage a very strong sacred-profane divide. Many converts find it difficult to part with lifestyles filled with deeply ingrained, doctrinally-justified practices, such as removing shoes upon entering the house to keep it pure, or praying at set times of the day using set rituals.

Continuing in a lifestyle similar to how they lived before the change in their beliefs, may lead to feelings of guilt because their day is structured around Muslim, not Christian, practices. But then they find that rejecting those practices leads to an emotional vacuum. Feelings of emptiness and guilt have to be addressed as they attempt to live out a belief system that does not have as great an emphasis on *tawhid* as that which they knew previously.

Perhaps the more common reaction among new converts, though, is the expectation that Christianity will offer them a new, similarly unified, lifestyle. These converts try to imitate everything about the Christians they know. This may involve choosing a provocative wardrobe, listening only to the same Christian music as their friends, or other lifestyle choices (which are often

---

[5] Numerous news articles about the controversies surrounding hijab and Islamic education in Turkey are frequently published. More than 80 years after Ataturk's death, the trend is reversing in Turkey, and there is now a growing movement toward Islamist reforms. See, for example, "Turkey: Erdogan's reforms: less schooling, more Koran", dated 24 February 2012, accessed at http://www.ansamed.info/ansamed/en/news/sections/politics/2012/02/24/visualizza_new.html_104136312.html, or "Ankara headscarf reform hot topic for Berlin's Turks", dated 8 February 2008, accessed at http://in.reuters.com/article/2008/02/08/us-turkey-germany-headscarf-idINL0675031720080208

remarkably liberal) based on the assumption that such practices must be critical to embracing a Christian faith.

It is also common for converts out of Islam to consider maintaining a number of Muslim rituals in their own lives for the sake of their Muslim friends and family. These converts struggle to know how to reconcile their recognition that rituals do not equate belief, with the sense that rituals have always been associated with belief in their families, and the anticipation that their new religious communities come with their own set of expectations. During my field research, I had on one occasion intended to give a participant some cherry liqueur chocolates as a gift to thank her for her time and willingness to share with me. The woman who had introduced us, a mutual friend, looked quickly at the box and snatched them out of the participant's hands before she could see what they were. I was surprised that this particular convert, who attends a Christian church regularly and whose daughters are being raised without any contact with their Muslim relatives, would still find alcohol offensive, but my gatekeeper assured me afterward that she had not made such a dramatic change in her life. In fact, even though she tried to isolate herself from her Muslim family members, she still frequently found herself in situations where she felt torn between her two lives and lifestyles.

Another participant explained to me the dilemma he faces every year when the fasting month of Ramadan begins. He told me that he recognises the value in fasting and told me that he does fast, sometimes during Ramadan and sometimes on other occasions. He wants to affirm the strong values demonstrated by his Muslim family members' commitment to fasting out of devotion. At the same time, though, he wants to assert the freedom he believes he has found in his new faith, and fasting during Ramadan might be seen by some to negate that freedom.

Every action for these participants still held a religious meaning, and a major element of their transition to a new faith was a constant process of negotiating which activities could be transferred and how, and which activities should be relinquished because they were expressions of their former belief systems.

Émile Durkheim's dialectic between the sacred and the profane is useful for conceptualising the role of *tawhid* in the lifestyle of so many members of Muslim communities. In any worldview, he argued, there is a natural and radical rejection of any relationship or association between what one defines as sacred and as profane (Durkheim 2001:39). In traditional Muslim practice, the sacred and the profane both abound, and the life of the devout is to be a constant endeavour to redeem the profane and bring it into the realm of the sacred. Every detail of life is religiously regulated, even the most mundane. What cannot be redeemed is ignored, or made invisible, because it can be a source of shame. One participant told me that when she was young her favourite room in the house was the bathroom, because she had been taught that God would not enter there. So she felt safe from his judgement when she was in that 'profane' space. Conversely, much that may be most easily traced to Arab or other local culture is also given religious meaning, thus ensuring unity.

When Muslims learn about Christianity, they generally encounter a different way of approaching life. According to the mainstream Western Christian doctrine most frequently taught to converts from Islam (different from the Orthodox Christian doctrine of most of the Middle East's Christian minority), there is a theological dualism, a tension between the other-worldly (transcendental) and the inner-worldly (immanent) (May 2003:112). In this worldview, the other-worldly is sacred, and the profane, or non-religious aspects of life, is simply left out of religious practice and instruction altogether.

What this means is that many converts from Islam to Christianity, most frequently a Protestant variation, are leaving a system where every intricate detail of life is dictated religiously, to one in which the sacred is held sacred, but s/he is given less orientation for the mundane details of life. This can cause confusion as a convert redefines his/her lifestyle.

One of the most complicated elements of living out *tawhid* as a convert to a Christian faith is the individual's expectations of how s/he will interact with Westerners. Arab Christians share many cultural traits with the dominant Arab Muslims in their countries, so they may be somewhat understanding of how converts in their midst may prioritise unity and community. Western Christians, on the other hand, usually come from much more individualistic cultures.

Even though they believe their decision to change religion is entirely faith-based, rather than driven by hope for material gain, many converts have expectations of missionaries or other Christians which Christian-background individuals feel are not justified but which are entirely logical in the light of *tawhid*. For example, young men often believe that their new faith will best be lived out if they are married to an American or European woman, not fully realising that Western Christians might then accuse them of converting in order to gain an American or European passport. These two motivations are simply not differentiated for many converts.

Many participants advised that it was important for Christian mentors to take a holistic approach to teaching and training new converts. One woman told me that her husband, who has been a Christian believer for several years, regularly evangelises and mentors people from a Muslim background. When they have accepted his message and he wants to start teaching them as young believers, he invites them to his home and feeds them, making sure to care for their physical needs before beginning to teach them from a Christian text. Participants often assured me that their faith decision could not be separated from the rest of their lives, that their jobs, families and everyday activities were influenced by their decision.

Based on the *tawhid* of God, the firm commitment to unity in Muslim communities creates a potential for high expectations of various other types of unity among converts to a Christian faith. This holistic perspective helps shed light on why the missionary contextualisation model so popular in missiological circles, whereby Muslims do not have to "convert" to Christianity in order to believe in Christ (Woodberry 2005:20), is problematic for many Arab Muslims (both MBBs and those in their surrounding milieu). It may be easier in non-Arab Muslim countries, or those without an established Christian community where national identity may be more easily separated from religious identity. But, in my research in a Middle Eastern context, many participants told me that they felt they would be somehow cheating or maintaining false ties to Islamic beliefs and to the Muslim *umma* (community, to be explored more in the coming chapter) if they were to continue to practice Muslim rituals. Some participants do continue living a Muslim lifestyle, but they assured me that it was somewhat deceitful, something they did merely for peace in their homes. Other participants deliberately ceased any activities construed as Muslim, such as prayer or fasting during Ramadan, when they decided to follow a Christian faith. If there was *tawhid* in their Muslim life, they cannot appropriate even a part of that to a Christian identity.

Umma: Perfect Community

Another application of *tawhid* is the unity of the community of Islam, the *umma*. It is an expression of the concept of *tawhid*, in that unity of the *umma* is held with utmost importance, and this sense of unwavering loyalty to the community is in fact one of the main constraints to conversion out of Islam. This chapter will discuss some of the implications of the idea of *umma*, and how it has often stood in tension with values like freedom of belief in Muslim societies.

The sense of demoralisation and threat that much of the Muslim world suffers in the light of the cultural and political dominance of the Christian West, has led to a perceived breakdown of the *umma*. If the *umma* cannot stand strong and proud, then its credibility, and by extension that of Islam, might suffer. This apprehension has led many Muslims to value the idea of a unified Islamic community even more, a sentiment which is, among other things, expressed in an inherent suspicion of outsiders, particularly foreigners and Christians.

An upbringing in a community where *umma* is held in such high esteem has a distinct impact on faith-changers' ideas about how their families will react to their decision, and on their expectations of their own new community.

Umma is a Type of Tawhid

The previous chapter discussed *tawhid*'s expression in the lifestyles of the faithful, and in the role of religion in politics and decisions made at the level of the wider society. Perhaps the most far-reaching application of *tawhid*, bringing with it the heaviest burden of expectations, is the unity of the worldwide Muslim community. Muslim anthropologist Akbar Ahmed writes, "The community or *ummah* is like the human body, the Prophet had said: If one part is in pain the whole body is in pain" (Ahmed 2003:46). Karen Armstrong suggests that everything about Islam is centred on unity of community: even the oral nature of Qur'anic recitation has served to enforce a group understanding of a shared community (Armstrong 2006:58).

The word *umma*, etymologically related to the word for "mother", captures the sense of a community that embraces and nurtures each of its members with utmost intimacy. The *umma* describes the sisterhood or brotherhood of the believers, the warm welcome extended to new converts to Islam or the unquestioning hospitality extended to fellow Muslims who have travelled far and are separated from their family. The unity of the community, expressed in *umma*, is seen as a communal expression of *tawhid*. It has come to mean a variety of other things as well, and is used in many different contexts, which has served to further emphasise its utmost importance (Asad 2003:197, Makris 2007:45).

Once again, history helps inform our understanding of *umma* in Islam. Before Islam emerged, Arabs were mainly loyal only to their tribal communities, but Islam brought a new type of allegiance which was more total than family ties: allegiance to the *umma*, or Islamic community. Working within the context of Arab culture, in which kinship was the centre of the social structure, Muhammad redefined kinship for the people who emigrated with him from Mecca to Medina. Most of them had found themselves cut off from their tribes, and some were even targeted for death by their tribesmen. Therefore, they became each other's kin, even for the sake of legal inheritance.

As Islam grew in political and social dominance, family and tribal ties were restored, and to this day families in the Arab world are generally very tight-knit. So while the *umma* did not replace family loyalty, it did become a community loyalty just as important to Muslims as kinship, or, for some, more so. In many communities, kinship and *umma* combined, resulting in an especially binding sense of loyalty to both family and faith.

The past few decades have seen several major encounters between Islam and the so-called "West", that is, the Christian and/or secular society that dominates Europe and America. The Rushdie Affair in 1989, in which many British spokespeople supported Salman Rushdie's publication of a novel which insulted Muhammad, *The Satanic Verses*, and the Danish cartoon incident of 2006, when a series of caricatures of Muhammad were published in a Danish newspaper, were both incidents in which Muslim communities all around the world felt deep offence at perceived disrespect from others. Furthermore, this disrespect seemed to be coming from a part of the world which was already economically and politically dominant. In response to these events, Muslims came together, standing unified in defence of their Prophet, even if this unity did not last. The sense of shame at the criticism levied at their leader inspired a greater drive to promote the importance of *umma*. Indeed, the narratives of history over the past century, with European colonial occupations, wars and economic development favouring the West, have accumulated, resulting in a sense of shame and humiliation that is shared by millions throughout the Muslim world: the whole *umma* suffers together (Makris 2007:45).

On the other hand, the famed attacks perpetrated by Muslims, of September 11, 2001, July 7, 2005 and others, took on a mystique in the minds of many Muslim communities. They already felt disadvantaged and threatened in a world favouring the West, and fear of retaliation exacerbated this growing sense of loyalty to *umma*. The West has been blamed for the disintegration of unity, but actually, there is a sense in which it is the shared idea of a common enemy that has grown out of these events, as well as war in Iraq, Bosnia,

Kashmir, Afghanistan and others. This shared sentiment has fuelled a sense of urgency to build unity among Muslims worldwide (Makris 2007:45).

Meanwhile, Muslim leaders have been promoting an image of "pure" Islam, a presentation of the way Islam was originally intended, that describes modern science and governance characteristics of the roots of Islam. In their narrative, the scientific endeavours of the Enlightenment reflected those of the great scholars during the Golden Age of Islam, so they argue that joining calls to modernity is a resumption of the progress that had been interrupted by traditionalism. This is part of a movement among Muslims to fight back the shame they feel at the hands of global politics and highly visible attacks on their Prophet, by claiming ownership of the structures of the West (Zubaida 2011:123). Such rhetoric is also framed as an insistent call for loyalty to the *umma*, for the worldwide community to stand unified against all others.

Social Unity over the Individual

The *umma* is defined by the equality of its members. The ideal *umma* would bring all Muslims from all different cultures and backgrounds together into an egalitarian community (Mernissi 2002:109). Although there are numerous obvious exceptions in practice, most notably the strong restrictions on women's rights still prevalent in many Muslim societies, there is a strong doctrinal tenet which teaches that each individual Muslim is to be assured of his/her full membership in the community and understand that this is his/her identity within the folds of Islam.[1]

At the same time, there is an understanding in many Arab Muslim communities that a strong *umma*, in which all members are notionally equal and none are distinct, will signify *tawhid* of the collectivity, which in turn makes possible a community at peace. "Renouncing freedom of thought and subordinating oneself to the group is the pact that will lead to peace; *salam* [peace] will be instituted if the individual agrees to sacrifice his individualism" (Mernissi 2002:89). Here emerges an important theme. The unity of the Islamic community is not simply a choice to not wage war against other members of the community: it has assumed a degree of surrender of one's individual identity and opinions for the greater good of the community. Mernissi suggests that a good Muslim may therefore be someone who obeys and sacrifices his/her own opinion for the sake of community (Mernissi 2002:40). She argues that the Arabic words for innovation and creation, *ihdath* and *ibda'*, have even come to connote negative and subversive activity.

---

[1] In an effort to assure full membership to each individual, some Muslim feminists have argued that perceived inequalities in Islamic law actually confer on women greater dignity, challenging the common understanding that women are worth less in Islam (Ahmed 1992, Nahle 1996, Bennet 2010).

Opposition of any sort to the shared beliefs and practices of the community is considered traumatic and frightening because it brings back the memory of violence in Mecca that preceded the emergence of a strong Muslim community and the years of peace that followed (Mernissi 2002:100). In part because the unity of belief and practices is so important in *umma*, many participants told me how they continue to attend mosque, wake up for morning prayers, or participate communally in religious activities, primarily to maintain the peace and unity in their Muslim communities. Indeed, if *umma* is important, then community is of crucial importance, and unity within the community is essential for maintaining unquestioning loyalty to the *umma*. For this reason, there is often a fair bit of expectation that members will conform to the priorities of the community: unity and community formation are easiest when there is homogeneity.

Ibn Khaldun wrote, "Social organisation is necessary to the human species. Without it, the existence of human beings would be incomplete" (quoted in Ahmed 2003:77). In discussing Ibn Khaldun's concept of *asabiyya* as an ideal type, anthropologist Akbar Ahmed writes, "When there is a conscious approximation of behavior to the ideal, at the different levels of family, clan, tribe, and kingdom or nation, society functions normatively and is whole" (Ahmed 2003:78). For Khaldun, group feeling is the fundamental basis for social order, and as such, lies at the very root of the rise and fall of societies (Zaidi 2011:94). For one who shares this perspective, society is seen as most functional and most stable when there is conformity of behaviour among its members. "The collapse of *asabiyya* also has sociological consequences. It creates conflict and violence in society. It sets one individual against another, one group against another" (Ahmed 2003:82). Khaldun suggested that God would only bring the ultimate consolidation and glory of Islam when the Muslim *umma* is united in *asabiyya* (Khaldun 1967:258). Failure to adhere to God's will, as manifest through social organisation, would result in the weakening of *asabiyya* (Zaidi 2011:96). As such, stability through social cohesion is held to be absolutely essential, a reflection of God's favour, but it comes at the cost of the freedom and privileges of individuals and minorities.

In keeping with this cultural and religious tradition, rejection of Islam is taken by many Middle Easterners to be a rejection of the Muslim community, and this is a key contributing factor to the problems faced by people who choose to embrace a Christian faith. Any group of people will naturally feel offended if its members abandon it, but a community whose very identity is built around its unity and cohesiveness is threatened at its very core by abandonment. One participant told me that this is why she avoids telling new Muslim acquaintances about her background. She prefers for them to think of her as simply an Arab Christian:

> In Arab cultures I have always wanted people to see me as Christian... I want them to know who I am now. Only when it's necessary to clarify, then yes, I will

> tell them about my Muslim family. Muslims don't usually continue the conversation after that. It is like I have betrayed their trust in some way. They have a sense of betrayal and pride: it's a shock, they're not really prepared for that. It's like, because I'm an Arab and they're Arab they feel like I'm one of them, but then when they find out we shared a religion, that should make us closer – but then I don't share that any more.

While her narrative illustrates her sensitivity to the feelings of Muslims whom she meets, many others, often young men, revel in the individuality they are experiencing for the first time, with an attitude that may resemble rebellion. They may expect that their decision brings with it a licence to independence from the *umma*. By making an autonomous life-changing decision, they develop a sense of rights and an expectation that their families should be granting them their individuality and freedom from community expectations. One man explained such a reaction to his family's expectations when they suspected he was deviating religiously: "If I stayed living in the family home [they wanted me to stop] going to church, hanging out with church guys, and telling stories about God stuff... But I kept going. When they asked me where I was going, I challenged them back. I would say, That's none of your business, or, am I still a little child that you question me?" To some extent, this defiant attitude may be linked with their understanding that they are affiliating with a religion that they associate with the West and modern values. But this insistence on individuality is also a function of a deeper choice to no longer conform to the rules of their community, in which the concerns of minorities are of secondary importance.

On the other hand, Mernissi points out, we must acknowledge that Islam did introduce a doctrine in which individuals were accountable to God for their own actions, to a community that had previously been marked by nomadic values whereby individuals had only existed as members of their communities (Mernissi 2002:93). Meccan society had apparently been in transition during Muhammad's lifetime from extreme communalism to increasing individualism. It was in that context that Muhammad, while emphasising the fact that an individual is responsible for his/her own acts, did also try to limit the excesses of individualism in the community. In other words, while Islamic doctrine does not deny the existence of the individual, for the sake of the *tawhid* of the *umma*, communal unity receives the greater emphasis.

Breakdown of the Umma

Many of the participants in this study emphasised that tolerance is very important to them. Some expressed irritation when their friends or family members were intolerant of their own or others' beliefs. As they made deviant, individualistic faith decisions, they came to value the ability for other people to do the same. Some people expressed sadness that their Muslim family members, particularly those women who were more secluded, did not seem to have any exposure to alternative ways of thinking, or did not feel the freedom to change their beliefs. When discussing how they would raise their children, despite their passion for their new-found beliefs, a number of people said that it was more important to them that they raise their children to think for themselves, than it was that they raise their children as Christians.

Various theorists of religion have suggested that as more and more people the world over are being exposed to other ideas and beliefs, their own worldviews are becoming increasingly relativised and hence tolerance for other belief systems is increasing.[2] There are many Muslims today who perceive globalisation as a challenge to Muslim *tawhid* and worry that the *umma* may be losing its power. While globalisation has in some ways brought Muslims together, it has not done so with such a great degree of unquestionable loyalty as it may have in the past. As long as all someone has known is Islam within a tight-knit community, it is easy to believe in the power of the *umma*. After that person learns about different faith systems, or different applications of his/her own faith system, it is much more difficult to maintain an unswerving belief that what s/he believes is the unquestioned and unquestionable truth, i.e. that there is "one true Islam" (Roy 2004:120). Many of the world's devout, whether they be Muslim or Christian or adherents to a different religion, increasingly find themselves challenged to defend the universality of their beliefs when talking with people from different traditions. As this is happening, maintaining cohesiveness in the *umma* is more and more difficult.

The response of many Muslims has been to begin to separate religion and belief, similar to separation of church and state in the West. More Muslims, especially those in fundamentalist movements, are emphasising the importance of "born-again believer" religiosity, in which their identity as Muslim by birth is different from their identity as a Muslim believer. As "born-again Christians" might do, these fervent Muslim believers may look down on the majority of Muslims who do not take their Islamic faith as seriously, or in the same way, as they do.

This struggle is being played out on a societal level, whereby Muslim believers are engaged in movements such as political Islam, but it is also happening at an individual level. Rejection of Islam is a choice that some Muslims make, just as others choose to become religious Muslims who are increasingly distinguished from the nominal Muslims that comprise the majority of their societies. However, there is still a sense that any act committed against the Muslim community is traitorous and shameful. Hence, while the majority of Muslims arguably see both fundamentalists and converts to Christianity or Secularism as a threat to the *umma*, they may express some degree of respect for fundamentalists but feel the need to repudiate apostates.

---

[2] See, for example: Beyer 1994, Heelas and Woodhead 2005

So it is that, while for some Muslims, globalisation and exposure has led to increased tolerance and even to changed beliefs, others have become more defensive of the idea of Muslim unity.

Freedom of Belief and Apostasy

Freedom of belief is highly controversial in many Muslim societies, and an understanding of the importance of *tawhid* and *umma* provides some insight into why there has historically been such unwavering condemnation of apostasy from Islam, a condemnation which has only in recent years begun to be questioned by Islamic scholars (Garces 2010, Davis 2011: 31-33). The importance of unity, particularly within the community, certainly makes it difficult to even consider leaving Islam, or more specifically a Muslim community. Someone learning about a different belief system might quickly conclude that it is best if his/her private beliefs are those which most support the larger community. It often seems that unity is best preserved by setting limits on individual expression and on privacy.

During the past century, Arab nationalist movements have introduced certain ideas of democracy, such as a constitution, parliament and suffrage, while avoiding ideas that in the Western interpretation of democracy are integral to running a democratic society, ideas like freedom of opinion and the sovereignty of the individual (Mernissi 2002:48). In Egypt, for example, there has long been widespread support for incorporating Islamic law, *shari'a*, into the national law, but the Mubarak government was extremely reluctant to do so. In post-revolution Egypt, one may argue that two distinct factions have emerged: the Islamist Muslim Brotherhood, who hope to institute a Muslim state, and a fiercely secularist youth movement which maintains that democracy in Egypt holds absolutely no space for religion. Neither option presents much support for the right to choose one's religion.

The tension between democracy and Islamic unity is illustrated through the 1948 Universal Declaration of Human Rights. The concept of freedom of religion, specifically the freedom to change religion, is protected by this document which was adopted by the United Nations General Assembly and is supported by most of the world's nations, but is actually understood by many Muslims as encouraging apostasy, a rejection of Islam which may include statements of blasphemy or theological differences. Apostasy may be a denial of Islam, but it is often perceived as being a denial of one's Muslim community, and as such may be taken as personal rejection by fellow community members. Accusations of apostasy are, therefore, not only about beliefs but are also, at least in part, an attempt to enforce unity in the *umma*, suppressing any dissent (Saeed and Saeed 2004:44-48,99-100).

Even though the leaders of many Muslim-majority nations perceived the Declaration of Human Rights as a challenge to the very foundations of Islam, possibly even encouraging apostasy and a return to the chaos that preceded

Islam (according to the dominant Muslim historical narrative), most Muslim nations signed it. They now find themselves caught between two contradictory sets of laws. While the Declaration grants freedom of thought, Islamically-justified traditions in many Arab countries have often condemned individual thought (Mernissi 2002:60). The solution has generally been to ignore the clause in the Declaration about freedom of religion, and to avoid educating the public about this freedom that they, in theory, have. It is easier to ignore the tensions caused by apostasy and freedom of belief, than it is to face them head-on.

The unresolved tension surrounding freedom of belief is beginning to open new debates. A variety of issues are now being put on the table, including people's involvement in certain community groups, the ability to choose their own political leaders, opportunities to debate and question Islamic doctrine, and the place for less-than-wholehearted adherence to Islamic law (Saeed and Saeed 2004:102,172). The greatest barriers remain, though, for individuals who may want to leave Islam, in that it continues to be expressly forbidden to leave the *umma* or to deny belief in the Muslim creed. Meanwhile, younger more-educated Muslims, especially in immigrant communities in Europe, are increasingly frustrated with their parents' unquestioning attitudes about religion, which they consider to be "traditionalism", instead seeking to understand Islam on their own. The result is actually often that they then choose a more conservative route than older generations have (Lewis 2007:65). So in communities where there is movement toward individualism, there is as often as not pressure toward greater conservatism in Muslim beliefs and rituals, further sidelining those who may desire to pursue a different route.

What has developed in many Arab Muslim communities is a reality in which individuals are taught that they are free to think and to develop their belief system, but only within very specific boundaries, most notably that they not leave Islam (Mernissi 2002:49). An apostate from Islam is deemed a traitor to the community because, while someone who has never known Islam may yet come to see its truth, the person who leaves has deliberately abandoned the truth, and the *umma*. But as long as one stays firmly within the *umma*, there is a great deal of space for diversity. The pillar of Sunni Muslim thinking is the existence of four separate schools of jurisdiction, each of which contains its own rules and interpretations of the Qur'an and *hadith*. This diversity in thinking is not only tolerated but celebrated. Similarly, I have met a number of communist Muslims, who are seen as somewhat different from others in their community but not suspected or accused of apostasy.

Until recently, the ban on apostasy went largely unquestioned in almost all Muslim communities.[3] This was arguably based on two sets of rationale. First

[3] There is a growing body of literature, both theological and legal, about Muslim apostasy and its consequences according to Muslim tradition and Islamic law. See, for example: Mawdudi 1994, Rahman 1996, Saeed and Saeed 2004, Garces 2010. This

the faithful assume that conversion to Islam is of benefit to the convert because it is the best way, and have no trouble considering conversion out of Islam to be a capital offence because, to them, it is clearly the wrong decision (Lewis 2003:48). Some also fear that, if Islam is no longer mandated among its adherents, then perhaps people will stop believing in God and the memory of the Prophet will dim (Mernissi 2002:65). The community's survival is seen to depend upon full submission to Islam.

Indeed, *tawhid* leaves no room for dualism, no option between full membership in the Muslim community and complete denial of the community. At the same time, though, we have seen that there is some space for freedom, as long as it is never verbalised or made visible to the community. Even if apostasy takes place in the heart and mind, in the realm of *belief*, it can only be accused or acknowledged if other people witness a blatant denial or mockery of Islam (Garces 2010:235). Indeed, for the sake of the *umma*, many communities will ignore signs of doubt or small acts of deviance.

It bears noting that, when individualism is discussed in a Muslim context, often what is meant is actually small-scale community instead of community on a societal scale, for example, placing family priorities over those of the larger Muslim *umma.*[4] Even though many apostates convert together with family members, or through intimate relationships, their religious change is still perceived by their community as being, on some level, a form of individual deviance. As conversion involves some type or degree of change in identity, regardless of how a person arrived at conversion, the identity issues and transformation faced by a religious convert are largely felt individually, even when the process of change is shared with other converts.

It is hard for many Western Protestant Christians to understand the *tawhid* of Islam that binds the individual to the community to such an extent that it affects his/her freedom of thought, both within and beyond families. Most Muslims who choose to embrace a Christian faith are attracted to Protestant doctrine, but continue to value their cultural heritage of communal cohesiveness above individual expression, and thus face a conflict of values between Christian individualism and Muslim communitarianism which is not necessarily related to their creed, though many converts may experience it that way.

---

debate, taking place in human rights communities and centres of Muslim theological thought, has significant sociological implications. Right now, most Muslims understand that apostasy is not allowed in Islam, and this contributes to the strong communal reaction against conversion out of Islam. If Muslim clerics and leaders of Muslim nations begin to change their approaches to this issue, the sense of communal shame that is presently associated with apostasy may also begin to transform.

[4] See Roy 2004 for a good illustration of this.

Expectations of the New Umma

People of a Muslim background who choose to follow a Christian faith were usually raised in the *umma*, and as this chapter has argued, leaving the fold of that *umma* is certainly not easy. The void left by loss of the Muslim *umma* will be addressed further in the coming chapter. After converting, they are looking for *umma* in their new community. They come into their new faith with high expectations of Arab Christians, very high expectations of missionaries and other people from Christian-majority countries, and particularly challenging expectations of what they should find in their life partner. I will not discuss the community of converts per se in this section, since with other Muslim-background converts there is already usually a shared understanding of *umma*. Each of these types of relationships will be further explored in the following chapters.

Expectations of Arab Christians

Most people from a Muslim background who choose to embrace a Christian faith desire a connection with the historical religion of Christianity. Most Middle Eastern countries, including Egypt and Lebanon, have large and influential Christian communities who trace their roots to the early days of Christendom. Converts who have had no previous contact with other people who share their faith are likely to look first to such Christian churches for community. Other people come to belief through the influence of a Christian, whether Arab or foreign, and so they connect their faith with Christianity. The few MBBs who do not automatically consider attending church usually made their decision due to the influence of a fellow convert who him/herself decided not to be involved in a church. As the number of converts is increasing, we can see the number of people converting due to the influence of a convert increasing, too, so perhaps fewer converts will choose to associate with Christian churches.

Among the participants of this study, though, most did seek out a relationship with a church, in the hopes of finding a new identity and a new community there. Belonging is important in the *umma*, and they were eager to reach a point of belonging to their new churches. In fact, sometimes converts even hope to be heralded and honoured in churches because of their choice, and it is true that converts in some places are welcomed, empowered and respected. Converts from Islam to Christianity in the United States or Europe are often asked to lead congregations or speak about their conversion experience. Converts to Islam in the West often similarly become leaders in Muslim circles. This is partially because they study their new religion carefully and become well-versed in theology, but it is also likely because their conversion contributes to the credibility of the religion (Haddad 2006:38-39).

Faith-changers who remain in the Middle East tell a very different story, though. They feel they are not respected by born Christians, especially not within the Christian churches that they begin to attend. One man explained that he would very much like to help with church ministries, to study and learn in order to eventually become a leader, but he has never felt as if the Christians want to listen to him: "The church does not care for us like it should. They would never think of having us serve in the church, but they really do love us and we feel very loved by church people, who come over and visit and look after us. But they don't ever really involve us, and they try to keep their distance." He emphasised that he had felt very welcomed by the church, and very loved by members of the church, but welcoming and love have not translated to trust: he does not feel that they trust him or that they could respect him. He does not feel he has become a full member of the Christian *umma*, which is what he hoped for.

Full membership in the Arab Christian *umma* would entail a reciprocal relationship. Converts would not only receive help, they would find opportunities to give help as well. A woman told a story of an experience that taught her not to expect an intimate relationship with born Christians. She became friends with a Christian woman who is her age, and they both had toddlers. The Christian woman helped her new friend quite a bit, often having her and her daughter stay over when her husband was travelling, and calling up frequently to see how they were doing. One day the Christian woman told her convert friend a personal secret in confidence, but then later told her that the information had been wrong. Eventually it got out that the secret had, in fact, been true. The convert woman felt betrayed because she understood that the Christian woman did not trust her, wanting to be the convert's confidante but unwilling to depend on her in return. The convert woman had been hoping for a true friendship and concluded that such a hope was in vain.

The failure to establish trusting relationships reinforces mutual suspicion between born Christians and Muslim-background converts, and many MBBs I met eventually reached the conclusion that they wanted nothing to do with Arab churches. In other cases, after the new believers have proven their commitment through years of loyalty to the church or through attracting more Muslims to change faith, relations have improved over time. Church relationships rarely seem to reach the quality of an *umma*, though.

Trust and suspicion is the most pressing concern facing relations between converts and Arab Christian churches. Believers from a Muslim background want to be welcomed into their new community, but Arab Christians are reacting to centuries of *dhimmihood*, the status of a minority in Muslim-majority nations. The Arab Christians suspect people of a Muslim background of having political or material motivations for converting, or worse, of infiltrating their churches as spies. Some participants told me that not even they have confidence that other converts will not return to Islam, so it is not surprising that some people who were born Christian would share that suspicion.

Nonetheless, converts made a difficult decision to follow the ideology of the minority, and when they are not respected, much less trusted, for that decision, the hurt they feel at the hands of Christians is often irrevocable. Too often, that feeling of hurt and suspicion extends to other converts as well, largely sparked by Christians' expression of their own suspicions, leaving MBBs craving *umma* and guidance as they forge the path of their new life.

A common term to describe the community of Muslim-background Christian believers is a "minority within a minority". This term describes them as a small group of Christians who are neglected for being a minority within the Christian community, which is itself a minority. The fact that legally, Muslims are not allowed to convert to Christianity in Arab countries, reaffirms this 'minority' status. No longer members of the Muslim *umma*, they can never be a part of the Christian *umma* either.

Expectations of Non-Arab Christians

Most converts actually see the missionaries they know as their religious leaders: they are respected believers and, unlike Arab Christians, they are often very interested in building relationships with converts out of Islam. As a result, MBBs are often more willing to take leadership from a foreigner than they are from an Arab Christian or from a fellow convert. In essence, this places the missionary upon a pedestal, with all the lofty expectations that this entails. Religious leaders in most Muslim communities are widely respected with a strong following, and new believers look to their new leaders with a similar degree of respect and willingness to follow.

This respect means that converts generally expect missionaries to act in a way that befits religious leaders and which demonstrates *tawhid*, with their actions affirming their words. In fact, since they have chosen a Christian faith over a Muslim belief system, they may expect that the quality of *tawhid* in the lives of missionaries will be greater than that which they saw in their Muslim leaders. They are looking for missionaries to do everything that is good, and to do it well. However, missionaries often do not achieve those expectations. One man explained his frustrations as follows:

> If you're not here to serve, it's better not to come at all. Serving means developing social relationships, visiting, living on the people's level. He has to have on his heart a desire for people to come to Christ, always ask, "How can I bring people to the message?" They can't be always concerned with the nicest clothes or getting a nicer car. People like that can't tell others to follow Jesus. At the same time, don't be a martyr – try to understand and live on the people's level. They need to try to help. It's not wrong to give someone who needs it $100, maybe do this up to ten times. No, not everyone will start to assume [they can take advantage of the rich foreigner]. There are people who need, who are really needy – they have no food and no clothes. After all, the missionaries came to serve people, there needs to be understanding, they need to be near people.

One commonly-cited expectation converts had of missionaries was that they demonstrate a great deal of generosity. In Arab tradition, the more a person has, the more a person gives, and s/he illustrates his/her wealth through the ability to be generous. In contrast to this cultural value, many missionaries deliberately try to separate their personal finances from their mission work, despite the relatively wealthy lifestyle they live in the Middle Eastern countries where they work. This is done in the spirit of a Western Protestant understanding of separation of church and state, or in this case, separation of ministry and personal. The missionaries' argument is that if they were to give money to the people they are evangelising, it would seem that they are trying to bribe them to be Christians. This causes some confusion and frustration since many, like the man quoted above, who could not understand why missionaries are so hesitant to give to the poor, are disappointed by the lack of care and the waste of resources they perceive in many missionaries. Indeed, many converts see that attitude as prideful and greedy, because they are viewing it from the perspective of *tawhid*: they wonder how someone can try to share a message without sharing the rest of his/her life?

At the same time, and creating a bit of a paradoxical situation, believers from a Muslim background are exerting their newfound individuality, eager to stand up for their individual rights and independence from *umma*. They look to missionaries, particularly those from Western Christian-majority cultures, to provide them with orientation as to how to live out their individuality. Unfortunately, though, they often find that they are objectified, put into a proverbial box with other converts, rather than treated as individuals. One young woman complained to me that when meeting with missionaries, they give the impression that they are repeating a message that they share with all of their Muslim-background acquaintances and do it in such a way that she suspects they are meeting with her merely in order to add a tick to the tally of MBBs they have encouraged. She sought friendship, but instead received the disappointing feeling that she is seen as no different from other people in her supposed community.

Most converts whom I met had been through a long and detailed process of coming to the conclusion that they could, and would, make a decision on their own that deviated from their community's expectations. They were now looking to missionaries to affirm that decision and to provide them with opportunities to practice this new skill of independent decision-making, but were also looking to missionaries to fill the void left when they lost their Muslim community's leadership structures. Missionaries often noticed that converts came to them seeking leadership and eagerly stepped into the role of mentor and guide, advising them what to do, but less frequently affirmed the autonomy of their new believer friends.

Perhaps most importantly, though, faith-changers from a Muslim background look to missionaries, their new community and religious leaders, to fill the void left by loss of *umma*. They are hoping to be welcomed into missionaries' homes and families, to share in intimate conversations and even secrets, to share holidays and special occasions. They are looking for the deep and intimate community that their families would have extended to a new Muslim in their midst.

Expectations of Spouse

Most of the participants I met converted before marrying, and several were still single when I met them. Finding an appropriate marriage partner was of paramount concern to them. Several of the young men said that not marrying was not an option for them, although some single women told me they would prefer to remain single if they could find a way to do that in their communities. Finding a suitable marriage partner is, for many MBBs, essential to their ability to live their lives in *tawhid*, developing an *umma* in their home, even if all other intimate relationships have broken down and no longer make sense. They believe that finding a partner who is sympathetic to their own beliefs, or, even better, shares them, will make it possible to continue with the same religious lifestyle. Several studies have confirmed that when marriage partners share the same religion, their church attendance figures are generally higher (Iannaccone 1990:303).

Such expectations are affirmed by the many stories of fulfilment told by converts who did indeed marry a fellow convert. In some instances their stories of marriage likened it to a second conversion, a discovery of a newfound freedom to participate in Christian religious activities and welcome Christians into their homes. On the other hand, participants who married people who did not share or support their beliefs often found it difficult to continue being as committed to practising their faith as they had previously, at least for a time. The effects of marriage on faith were especially accentuated for women. Marriage can have a significant effect on how someone lives the rest of his/her life, either affirming a new identity, or else ending a season of individuality and forcing one back into the Muslim community.

Men have more choice in marriage, since legally they can marry a Muslim, a Christian, or even a Jew, though a non-Muslim choice of wife is frowned upon in many communities. They also generally take a leadership role in their homes, and so if they marry someone who does not share their faith, they have the freedom to continue with their Christian involvement, and often they lead their wives to convert as well. A few single men said that they would ideally marry an MBB, or alternately a Christian woman. If all else failed, they would marry a Muslim woman. Muslim women, on the other hand, can only legally marry Muslims, so if they want to marry someone who shares their Christian faith, they must marry a fellow convert. Some women get married in the West, and a few find ways to manoeuvre around the law to marry a Christian, but many look desperately for an MBB husband or concede to marry a Muslim man.

Most male participants told me that they find, or found, choosing a life partner extremely challenging, and that they were usually looking in the midst of strong family pressure to wed. Many of them reported several refused proposals, and a sense of desperation that they might not find someone suitable and so be convinced to marry a good Muslim girl chosen by their mothers. However, most stories of MBB men who married Muslim women who did not share their Christian faith have ended in relative happiness, with the convert continuing to freely follow his new faith. I met a few women who had actually converted through the influence of their husbands, and one man told me that after three years of marriage, his wife became very interested in his faith and was reading the Bible regularly. Even before they were married, she had already accepted that his faith was different, and so he remained consistently active at church and he was the one making the decisions about their son's religious education. So it may be that some of the stress and pressure that single convert men feel to find the perfect spouse, is somewhat unfounded, since marriage to a Muslim woman may not necessarily be a threat to their faith in the way that they fear.

For many of these men, though, the desire to pursue the perfect marriage is something that comes with their decision to choose their own faith community. One missionary told me that the most significant difference he sees between his Muslim and his MBB friends is their attitude toward marriage. It is said in Islam that marriage completes a person, and that building a good family is a religious obligation, essential to becoming a good Muslim. Marriage becomes more of a religious rite than an act of love. When the Muslims this missionary knows embrace a Christian faith, they become more interested in developing a friendship with a woman and marrying for love. Convert men, as a result, are looking for a woman who can both complete them religiously, and with whom they are in love. In marriage, they want it all, and those who marry someone who does not fulfil all of that may feel like they are settling for less, even if living in relative happiness.

Because of the emphasis placed on marriage in many Muslim communities, it can also solidify a man's position in his family and help ease the tension that ensued from his conversion. It proves that he is at least somewhat stable and respectable, with at least some sense of the importance of *umma*. One man told me that, even though his family was not happy with his choice of a Christian wife, his relationship with his parents improved significantly after he was married, and even more so after he had children.

Women find themselves in a different situation. A number of women have no option other than to marry a Muslim man. Even if a woman maintained her reputation and relationships in her community when she converted, if she marries a Christian man she may then be seen as an apostate. Indeed, marrying a Christian is not even perceived as an option for many. One woman spent many years hoping to marry a convert, but finally gave in and married a Muslim man. Since her marriage, even though her husband had known about her faith from the beginning and told her he accepted it, he pressured her to start wearing the *hijab* again and she has had little opportunity to be with Christians. After hearing stories like hers, many women converts are eager not to marry a Muslim, do not see how they can marry a Christian, and so look for an MBB for as long as they can withhold family pressure to marry at an appropriately young age.

So far it has been very difficult for convert women to meet MBB men whom they can marry, even more so when considering the strong desire of many convert men to fall in love and feel a deep connection with the woman they marry. For single MBB women, though, marriage to a man "like her" is a ticket to freedom, so many of them are eager, nay desperate, to meet MBB men. This in some way complicates their hopes: many male participants reported that the convert women they have met demonstrated such an eagerness to get married and escape the restrictions of their home, that they seemed little interested in building a relationship or marrying for love, an attitude the men found utterly unattractive.

In spite of this, I have encountered very few stories in which two converts marry and then later regret their decision, regardless of how strongly love and passion weighed in the decision. As religious deviants surrounded by a strongly cohesive society, a shared culture and a shared faith often dim many of the potential strains on their marriage, which are frequently experienced by people who marry born Christians or still-Muslims. There is *tawhid* in the marriage, which matters a great deal.

A Perfect Dream

Taking into consideration the context from which many MBBs come, as described in previous chapters, I will now explore that to which they are turning. This will be discussed in terms of the process and challenges involved in adapting their lives according to their new faith. The challenge of adapting to a new identity is excruciatingly difficult because the picture they had of a life in the folds of a Christian faith is so often intensely different from the life they encounter. This chapter is about the dreams converts have about their lives, and the frustration and disappointment that they feel when they break with those dreams.

Christianity is a Known Element

Several times in my research I met men who had for a time been very interested in Christianity but knew nothing about how it is practised, nor knew any Christians. Many of these men went first to the nearest Christian church looking for someone who could satisfy their curiosity. One man, for example, dreamed repeatedly of Jesus and eventually decided he wanted to go to a church to learn more. He had no Christian friends so had no way of gaining an introduction; as a result, people at the church were suspicious and turned him away, but he kept trying to meet Christians. By the time he was finally able to make the connection with Christians, his family had learned of his dreams and used extreme measures, including kidnapping and violence, to convince him to change his mind. His story evokes two observations about the relationship between Christian doctrine and the historic religion of Christianity: first, that it was one man's impulse to look for Christianity based on dreams of Jesus; and second, that his family immediately associated his interest in Jesus with the historic religion of Christianity, even though they had had no prior direct contact with churches or Christians.

It is essential to note that a discussion about Muslim conversions to Christ, or Christianity, is about an affiliation to an element that is already somewhat-known in the Arab world, especially the countries of the Middle East. This is an encounter between two world traditions that have a long history of co-existence and conflict (Jenkins 2002:34). Converts between the two religions are entering a history of polarisation between the world's two largest religious traditions (Wohlrab-Sahr 2006:74). Christianity and Christians are hardly unknown in Arab Muslim society, particularly the nations of the Middle East such as Lebanon and Egypt, even though many Arab Muslims like this man and his family, have had little or no personal contact with Christianity or Christians.

Different Muslims in the Arab world have different perceptions of Christianity, but all have deeply ingrained ideas about what Christianity is. For example, one participant in this study told me that her family was upset with her interest in Christ and the Bible because they saw that as an affiliation with a rival political faction. But another participant, who worships in the same church with her, was a communist before converting: he told me that his family was more accepting of his communist leanings than of his later Christian association, because communism was considered a political, not religious, association. Though the motives for their reactions against Christianity were different, both families had strong, deeply ingrained, concerns.

Christianity is, for most Muslims, the "other". Even where a historic Christian community has thrived for the past two millennia, it is somehow tied to Europe and America. The narratives of history have defined perceptions and relationships in many communities of the Middle East, and the history of Muslim-Christian relations in the Middle East includes a number of narratives that still resonate in Arab communities today. Dating back to the beginnings of Islam, the Muslim world has had contact with the Christian world, and that contact has often been conflictual.

In the Middle East, the spread of Islam in the seventh and eighth centuries broke the rule of the Byzantine Empire, which had held a strongly Christian hegemony over the region for centuries. This hegemony had already been weakening and the Arabs were newly unified under Islamic rule. At first Arab Christians and Arab Muslims interacted well, and many Arab Christians held an important role in the new Muslim administration (Sahas 1991:7). As the Islamic power base increased, however, Arab Christians became more of a distinct minority and felt the pressures that came with minority status. Even at this early point, the tensions between Christians and Muslims in the Middle East were not based on theological doctrine nor religious practice so much as a power struggle between two theocratic communities (Sahas 1991:17). Most contemporary Middle Eastern Muslims are in fact descendants of Christians in the region who converted to Islam during that era, opting to leave their faith for a religion that brought with it a political affiliation with the Muslim community, a community with whom they felt a strong ethnic and cultural affinity (Ayoub 1991:174). In contrast, those who remained Christian may today still prefer to identify primarily with a pre-Islamic ethnic group and only secondarily as Arab; for example, many Lebanese Christians describe themselves as Phoenecians and Egyptian Coptic Christians may say that they are ethnically Coptic.

Probably the most famous historical encounter between Christianity and Islam was the series of Crusades in the eleventh and twelfth centuries, when for a brief period of time European Christians occupied and ruled parts of the Middle East. Though sentiment among Muslims about Christians at the time was mixed, and largely based on questions of convenience, most of the Muslims who fought in the Crusades not only despised "the Franks" but saw their struggle against Christian rule as a fight for God. The image of the Crusades which remains in the consciousness of much of the Muslim world today is one of Western Christian brutality, taking advantage of a position of dominance (Curry 2002:38).

More recently, the Muslim world is emerging from two centuries of European colonialism. Colonisation in the Middle East is often associated with Christianity, not only because the colonising nations were Christian-majority, but also because they often brought with them an aggressive Christian missionary movement. This experience refreshed the negative impressions of Christians in Muslim consciousness (Michel 1997:62, Makdisi 2008). Few modern-day missionaries recognise the emotions and resulting sensitivity that underscore their attempts to convert Muslims. The potential for conflict is further increased because both Islam and Christianity are openly missionising religions which claim a universal message (Jenkins 2002:168).

In recent centuries, the "West" has been associated by many people in the "East" with trade and political dominance, and with Christianity, which is in turn associated with secularism – non-religious and anti-religious thinking such as the writings of the Enlightenment. The "East" is conceptualised as being more religiously diverse, but with a very strong Muslim heritage, and the times and places where "East" and "West" have met, have also been a meeting of Christians and Muslims. Though many Muslims claim to respect religious Christians, they find it hard to trust a religion that is represented by societies that have rejected faith in favour of science. Saeed and Saeed similarly argue that, though there have been few Christian converts in historically Muslim lands, "the success of Westernization leading to secularization among many Muslims there is seen by many Muslims as an indirect 'Christianization' of their societies" (Saeed and Saeed 2004:109).

At the same time, many Muslims in the Middle East actually have a rather mystical perception of Christianity, particularly but not exclusively Eastern Christianity. Christian shrines are places of miracles, and Muslims and Christians alike will often go to Christian shrines for healing. One participant in this study said that many Muslims believe that the church has power. On one hand, she was taught to fear that power and to believe that a church could kill her at will; on the other hand, because of this belief, it was to a church that she went when she was searching for a job.

Arab culture should be held as distinct from Muslim culture, but historically there has been a great deal of overlap. It is in many ways quite different from European culture, and dialogue between East and West, Christian and Muslim, is frequently tainted by faulty assumptions and understandings on both sides. Though many Arab nations appear to have adopted many of the patterns of modernity imported from Europe, in areas such as commerce and technology, this has not been followed by a meeting of the minds, except for within a small slice of an Arab urban middle class which has advocated for an interpretation of European-style secularisation (Watenpaugh 2006). The events of the Arab Spring seem to be giving that small slice a louder voice and greater realm of influence, but they are still few in number and far from representative of the opinions of their wider communities.

As Muslims come into contact with Christians, and vice-versa, it is hard for people to separate themselves from their society. This is especially true in confessional societies, found in much of the Middle East, which have a long history of coexistence. In these countries, especially, one's religious identity is an intrinsic part of one's overall identity. Though inter-religious conflict happens and receives quite a bit of media attention, regular day-to-day contact between Arab Muslims and Arab Christians is generally peaceful, and there is a degree of mutual respectful distance. For example, Muslims will work on Easter and Christmas, and Christians during Eid al-Fitr and Eid al-Adha, so that each can celebrate his/her respective holy days. This is a fragile balance, though, and one that is easily disturbed by acts of religious deviance, such as individual decisions to convert across religious lines. Though Arab Christianity often looks quite different from expressions imported from the West, it is still generally recognised as the same religion.

The perception of a religious community as voluntary and faith-based is seen as inherently a Western individualistic concept, in contrast with the high value Arab, and most Muslim, cultures place on family and community commitment. Movements toward greater individualism in faith and religion are often blamed on foreign, that is European or American, influence (Tamadonfar 2001, Roy 2004:39). To the extent that European expansion and success have overshadowed the rich heritage of the Arab world, there is a strongly felt need among many Muslim Arabs to struggle against the encroachment of such foreign influences. Most of the participants in this study grew up in families that feel strongly about these religio-political tensions. While these Arab MBBs may not have left Islam and pursued Christianity out of political motivations or a desire to become "Western", they understand that this is, to some extent, exactly what they have done. Their faith decision is inseparable from the societal and political issues surrounding Muslim-Christian relations in their home communities, and in their own consciousness.

The Attraction, not the Motivation

In conversion literature, there are several elements involved in the process of redefining identity. One theme has been biographical reconstruction, or redevelopment of a personal narrative, to develop a convert identity (Snow and Machalek 1984, Sremac 2010). This process often involves placing pre-conversion life events into what may be referred to as an "attribution scheme", a discovery of the meaning of their life path, and a recognition of who they were all along (Staples and Mauss 1987:135-137). In this way, a convert does not see his/her life as beginning anew at conversion, but instead sees conversion as an event that consolidates his/her identity throughout life.

Several participants told me that they had had experiences early in life that, as they look back, they came to understand as anticipating their change. One woman told me that she now understood how all the events in her life, many of which she had previously seen as tragedies, made sense to her as she grew into her new identity:

> It all made sense to me now – why we had come to [this country], why I had to be from a poor Sunni family, all of it – it all came together for me in order for me to meet Christ. Maybe if I had been rich I wouldn't have known him... I strongly believe there are no coincidences in life. I studied accounting, but now I teach Arabic – for a while I wondered why, but now I realise why – I learned how to write and type in colloquial Arabic, and now I am working writing [Bible-based] stories in colloquial to be recorded on tapes used for witnessing. It all makes sense.

Her account was particularly detailed in how she saw various events in her life coming together to comprise one larger attribution scheme. Many people attributed a similar role to minor events in their lives. Another woman, for example, told me that her friends at school had all teased her because her physique was similar to that of a Christian girl; now, she sees that as a sign from her childhood that she was meant to be Christian. Another man told me of many thoughts he had that were not his own, including an ability to tell Bible stories that he had never heard before, well before he ever saw a Bible. When he went to a church and met a priest, it all made sense to him.

Muslim converts to Christianity are often accused of converting because they want things that the West is known to offer: wealth, visas, educational and employment opportunities, etc. In this research, I found almost no evidence to support such a claim even when these things did follow, or even were anticipated. Each individual I spoke with went through an intellectual process of considering Christian doctrine, and an experiential process that emotionally supported their conversion process. That being said, many converts have hopes, even expectations that, as a result of their decision, they will gain access to some of those Western privileges that they have long associated with Christianity. It fits conveniently into their attribution scheme.

When people make a decision to follow a new faith, they do so with high hopes for their possibilities, and with the expectation that this will give them fully realised lives. Indeed, one of the great appeals for many Muslims who were considering Christianity, was the freedom it gave to its adherents to live their lives according to their own conscience, without Islam or their community dictating their lives.

As they make more Christian friends, especially American and European friends, this expectation grows, for some it evolves into a demand. After all, their Christian friends describe the freedom and respect they themselves enjoy, and, coming from families where *tawhid* and *umma* were so important, many converts desire the same freedom and respect which they come to see as an integral part of the *tawhid* of a Christian faith. One young man explained why his dream is to go to the United States:

> I used to think it's easy to someday have my own company [here], maybe be a manager one day. Now I realise that no, it won't happen... My American friend... told me that in the U.S. everyone is equal. I could work there as a normal employee if I am respected! [He] also told me that I could make even ten times as much there than I make here... Also, if I go, I want to be on a mission against Muslims. They make you pray, fast, read the Qur'an; because of Islam, there's huge community pressure, which I hate. It causes a lot of frustration.

This poignant quote captures a great deal of sentiment. There is a contrast drawn between Islam and Christianity, home and the "West", whereby he perceives Islam as the religion of rules and restrictions and pressure, but in America he will be free to speak his mind and respected as an individual, a Christian individual. America has captured his imagination as the place where he can be a true Christian and speak in opposition to Islam. Furthermore, the prospect of wealth has been incorporated into this dream. He describes the United States as a type of Christian utopia, and credits his American friend with introducing him to the dream. While few participants were so descriptive and direct, his sentiment was reflected in many interviews, especially with young men who did not have strong family obligations or attachments at home. Many, especially women, lose everything when they assert their freedom to leave the *umma*, and they turn to Christians to support them in this newfound freedom cum loss.

Westerners and Western Money: Missionaries and the Dream

Christian ministry projects are largely funded with Western money. Most of the evangelical and protestant churches in the Middle East are primarily financed from other countries, with a nominal contribution only coming from the church members themselves. Other projects for community outreach, including schools, social centres, and health clinics, are almost exclusively funded with Western money, sometimes through charitable donations and sometimes they are paid for by local Westerners, for example for Arabic studies. This is particularly prevalent in Lebanon.

Many converts are invited to work at these projects, and some Muslims who work, or who benefit from, them, are attracted to learn more about Christ through contact with the Christians, usually Westerners, who they meet through these venues. This has proved to be an effective model of attracting Muslims to consider a Christian faith, but it has also strengthened an already-present association between Christianity, the West and wealth. Whether it is openly stated or not, the beneficiary community is usually well aware of the funding source. In one case, a project was shut down and the Westerners all left after an incident occurred putting the project staff at risk. The Muslim women who worked there and who benefited from the project, and who had been seriously considering conversion, were left behind. For them, they had not only been abandoned materially, but through that, they had been abandoned spiritually.

After a person makes a decision to follow a Christian faith, new opportunities arise. When individuals are forced out of their homes or face legal harassment because of their decision, Christians, usually Western Christians, sometimes help them, occasionally even sponsoring their immigration to a Western country. There are also extensive efforts to support new believers in the Muslim world by sponsoring theological training, international gatherings at which converts can meet with each other, media training for Muslim-background believers in Christ to engage in evangelistic activities using on-line or broadcast media, and various other such initiatives. From the perspective of Christian churches, it is very honourable to support fellow believers, and it is strategic in the interests of expansion to help them become more effective at spreading their new beliefs within their communities. Furthermore, without outside support, many converts would suffer drastic consequences as religious deviants in their communities. However, these efforts also serve to confirm a growing sense that the land of the Christians, the West, where freedom and wealth reign, is now within their reach. Again, this study did not reveal evidence to suggest that this is the motivation behind most people's conversion decision, merely that this access is often an outcome, and it was expected.

Participants had some firm warnings for missionaries with regards to this. One woman told several stories about missionaries she knew enjoying comfortable lives and shamelessly flaunting it in front of their Muslim and convert friends. In fact, she knew some converts who started going to Western restaurants and spending more money, money they did not have, on family entertainment because they were following the example of the Western Christians that they knew. She recalled that as a young believer she was impressionable and eager for guidance as to how to shape her new life, and she knows that many converts follow the example of Western Christians carefully because they are trying to understand how to be Christians. She went on to say:

> They are often living so high. They don't look like missionaries. My idea of missionaries is that they are supposed to be humble, to care, not be rich, or at least not show it. They say they are something but you see something different. They're on a mission for God, and they should act like it. God on earth was poor – he gave up everything to live here. His message to his followers was, If you have two coats, give one of them away, Feed the poor… Too many missionaries don't show a picture of Jesus Christ – or not a complete picture, anyway.

Her warning was echoed by many of the participants who had converted several years previously, that is, who might be considered more mature. They were concerned that missionaries are bringing the wrong message, and that they are wasting precious resources. Many missionaries in these narratives were described as doing nothing noteworthy by way of ministry projects, but taking a large salary and living in a nice home, sending their children to nice private schools, in order to do this. This causes frustration among the more experienced or pensive believers, and causes confusion among less mature converts as to what it actually means to be a Christian.

Another man acknowledged that other missionaries do indeed set a good example through good works, saying, "There are two types of missionaries. One are those who spend money, and the others send the message, and live it. With the first type, we don't benefit at all – if they just sent the money here, it would help... But then there are others who live a simple life and serve. I know a lot, one is a Filipino pastor here, but he works a job, and he serves. He came to serve, but he's working, too." Indeed, most of the examples of missionaries who lived sacrificially, demonstrating generosity toward the people they were serving, came from outside of the United States and Europe, that is, outside of the "West".

A distinction was made between "Western" missionaries and those who come from other regions, in terms of both their employment status and their generosity toward people who were less well-off. It would be unfair to suggest whether this distinction is related more to converts' perceptions or expectations of people from different parts of the world, rather than to inherent differences in culture and values of generosity. However, many Western missionaries have told me that they deliberately try to separate their personal finances from their mission work, but non-Westerners, including Arabs, are often less concerned with this segregation. As a result, many converts see a lack of care and waste of resources in the choices of many Western missionaries. Most missionaries from non-"Western" countries cannot afford to depend on support from their home countries alone, and so they work jobs in the local economy as well. Finances that made sense to members of their Arab communities helped assuage many of the concerns and doubts. A few different participants made a point of recommending that missionaries work paying jobs and minister in their free time, not only to ensure financial integrity, but also in order to be able to relate better to the lives of the people they serve.

The participants who vocalised these concerns were not recommending that missionaries take a vow of poverty. Many know missionaries who had done this, and these participants watched as government suspicion turned on them and impoverished neighbours started to try to take advantage of them. Rather, they were looking for missionaries to live in a financially transparent manner, with open arms both materially and emotionally. Born Christians are their new *umma*, and they want their *umma* to live up to the hopes and expectations that they hold for their new life.

Unfortunately, the actions of Western missionaries have been taken as a standard for many Arab Christians and converts in the Middle East. One woman told a heartbreaking story of missionaries from her home country who were working in another Arab country, where she too was working at the time. Though they had met her and knew that she was a new believer in Christianity, they kept their distance from her. As best she could tell, they kept their distance because they were busy sending their children to nice schools, shopping and setting up a nice home. This culminated at Christmastime when they asked her to leave them alone so they could celebrate as a family. Another man found that, as a convert, he was caught up in a competition over money:

> I know many pastors are in their position just to get money. Once there were two people fighting over me; they each wanted me in their group because I'm a convert. And then one of them told me that the other was trying to get me in his group because he would get more money. This time, these were [people from my country]. Too many people who minister here have a nice life, they don't go to where the people are poor. They speak about the Lord, but they don't live it.

Do No Harm

Muslim converts to a Christian faith often develop a set of desires that, like *tawhid*, extends well beyond a change in thinking. This is not the whole story. Most people who convert do so earlier in life, and as they mature both emotionally and in their knowledge of their new faith, they realise that these dreams are unrealistic and develop more likely dreams. They dream of family, of acceptance for what they believe, and of opportunities to share their faith with other Muslims. This will all be discussed further in the following two chapters, but first I want to suggest that a certain caution by born Christians can help keep unrealistic dreams in check.

There are risks in the missionary enterprise. Many of these are well-known, especially as the media creates an image of terrorism and animosity in Muslim countries. Missions groups are careful to protect their email correspondence, their online identities, their phone calls, and their relationships. They hesitate to tell people in Muslim countries what they are doing there until a certain level of trust has been established. Stories of imprisonment and expulsion have affirmed the appropriateness of such precautions.

Many of the participants in this study, however, were personally offended by missionaries taking such precautions. MBBs themselves often need to be willing to sacrifice and take on increased risk in order to welcome missionaries into their lives. Several participants mentioned that their neighbours and friends observe their social comings and goings. If they are seen with foreigners very frequently, this can raise concern that they are involved in illicit activities. Usually the concern is not inherently religious in nature, rather they are suspected by their neighbours of supporting Western political causes, possibly engaged in espionage. Nonetheless, considering the *tawhid* of society in many Arab Muslim communities, such suspicions put the converts at risk.

One participant told a story of a time she was invited to the home of an American family. They invited her and a number of other Arab friends to what turned out to be a rather large party. This young woman had not been aware that her hosts were missionaries, nor had she been aware that such a diversity of people would be invited. Later she learned that a photo of her which was taken at that party, was on file at the local security office: among the people they had invited, at least one informant had been spying on the missionaries and their circle of contacts. When she eventually learned the Americans' reason for being in her country, the young woman felt that they had personally put her at risk. Had she known they were missionaries, she would have been more cautious in accepting their invitation and wary about staying at a party with so many people whom she did not know. From the American family's perspective, however, their status in that country was on a need-to-know basis, and the fewer people who knew them as missionaries the better.

Since *umma* continues to be important to so many converts, they are often very eager and willing to open up to missionaries, making themselves vulnerable in a relationship where the vulnerability is not reciprocated. This young woman's hurt probably had more to do with her hurt in realising that they had not opened up to her, than it did with the fact that their caution put her in danger's way.

Other participants warned that foreigners do not understand the context or the culture well enough to avoid making mistakes that may cause more harm than good. One man explained, "In our culture, some people lie; it's ok in our culture... But I, from in the culture, I know what is a passable lie and what is a non-passable, big, lie. A foreigner won't know the difference. I was raised in this culture... people can't pull it off on me like they can on a foreigner." Some participants told stories of times that they had accepted help or advice from missionaries that had ended up causing them bigger problems in the long-run. One specific type of risk is when outsiders put people in touch with each other or tell people things about other people they know. As I will discuss in the following chapter, people with a problematic secret, like most converts in the Arab world, depend on their ability to control the flow of knowledge about themselves.

I cite these observations because among born Christians working in the Arab world, especially foreign Christians, there often seems to be an understanding that the mere presence of Christians is of advantage: God will open up doors for conversations and evangelism, and the important thing is to be available when these doors open. Stories told by participants in this study indicate, however, that it is simply not that straightforward.

Over the course of half a century of humanitarian aid, bringing life-saving essentials such as food and shelter to victims of natural disasters and conflicts, instances began to emerge in which the aid and the manner in which it was provided contributed to community problems or to social divisions, ultimately causing more harm than good. In 1999, Mary B. Anderson published a book called *Do No Harm: How Aid Can Support Peace – or War*. With this book she began a movement among aid agencies to consider the various aspects of their work, the social context in which they are working, and a number of other factors, to determine areas in which they may inadvertently do harm, or, with a minor tweak, contribute to long-term peaceful development.

Do No Harm has captured the imagination of aid workers all around the world, and is a mantra for their desire to help people in the ways that will truly help, and avoid causing more problems through misguided attempts. Such a mindset seems morally responsible for any group of people attempting to impact a community for good, particularly missionaries whose primary aim is to bring what they believe is good news to people who might benefit from it.

In keeping with this principle, I here suggest specific questions that missionaries, Arab Christians, and more-experienced converts, might need to consider if they are truly committed to doing no harm, rather contributing to the perfect dream, in their work with Muslims and converts from a Muslim background: *Are relationships being strengthened such that the Christian umma is increasingly resilient? Do converts and potential converts have an opportunity to consider doctrine and also to experience something that will emotionally draw them to a new faith? Are assumptions about Christianity openly addressed? Do Christians acknowledge the things about their faith that are Western, without giving the impression that the West equates Christianity? Is the dream of individualism affirmed, or is it challenged? Do new believers have an opportunity to consider the freedoms they might or might not have in their new faith, in relation to their responsibilities if they desire to be morally upright people? Are local cultural assumptions considered when making choices about employment and financial management? Is there an open dialogue about what privileges may be afforded to new believers, and to what end? Do converts have sufficient autonomy to determine their own risk factors and respond accordingly?*

I do not propose answers to these questions, and my research has revealed little by way of universal solutions: the answers will often be different for each individual and location. Other questions can surely be added and/or adapted to a specific context.

Anomie

Religious converts often start out with a sense of optimism when they first embrace their new lives, but reality sets in as they come to acknowledge what they left behind. Frustration results as their new experiences fail to live up to the expectations that they had. This frustration can be seen as an expression of anomie. “Anomie” is a term which has held a variety of meanings and uses throughout the history of both Sociology and Psychology, and so it can be used to describe a variety of different identity struggles. The definition that I use here is based on a concept first explored by some of the older literature on anomie, the sense that one sees a glimpse of something more, and sets his/her hopes on attaining it, but is frustrated by an inability to achieve it (Durkheim 1952, Sennett 1998, Downes and Rock 2003:111).

Anomie is often a result of normlessness in society, a lack of structure and regulation, which leads to a breakdown of moral values (Durkheim 1952:252). Though anomie is often used to refer to a societal condition, it is also often experienced as a highly personal feeling, something mainly psychological, that results from one's expectations of and interactions with society (Rose 1966:37). Most theories of anomie focus on explaining how anomie can lead to crime and deviance, but here I explore the anomie that results from a highly idealised deviant decision.

According to Durkheim in *Suicide*, when a person develops a goal or expectation in life that is by definition unobtainable, s/he may be condemning him/herself to unhappiness. Therefore, s/he is either always looking for more, or else gives up (Durkheim 1952:248, Downes and Rock 2003:109). For example, Robert Merton described anomie in the United States during a period of strong economic growth, as a result of a season in which people's wealth and possibilities grew tremendously and they were encouraged to be ambitious. The means by which people could most effectively reach their goals, however, were not necessarily culturally acceptable, nor always legal (Merton 1968:189). He characterised anomie as a result of "imperfect coordination" of goals and means within a social structure: a confusion related to the conflict between value systems, a complete deterioration or even disintegration of those value systems (Merton 1968:213-217). More recently, anomie has been described as a fall-out of globalisation: as people come into contact with other religions and ideologies, it is easier to catch a glimpse of possibilities and it is harder to ignore inequalities between people (Kelly 2010:11, Zajda 2011); furthermore, identities and societal structures are less stable, contributing to increased anomie (Milner et al 2011). The "rules of the game" are no longer clear, so social stability is easily disrupted. This disruption is necessary for society to change, but it can also lead to deviant behaviour and a sense of anomie among many (Braithwaite 2010:18). Some research has indicated that the more individuality (for example, unmarried men without family commitments), the greater the anomie (Cao et al 2010:635).

In a society in transition, people's lives may fall into a routine after a season of excitement about a bright future, and opportunities do not materialise as hoped. The resulting frustration is captured in the image of a young man who attends university with a sense that he can be anything he wants, but twenty years later he realises that his drive for success has led him to instability and a loss of the moral values by which he was raised. He may experience anomie, in the form of irritation, self-disgust, normlessness, individualism and, often, an inclination toward deviance (Sennett 1998:31, Downes and Rock 2003:110-115, Baron 2011:227).

This understanding of how social disruption can lead to feelings of anomie can help describe the lives of religious converts in the Middle East, for two reasons. First, conversion is in and of itself a form of social deviance, and so the feelings of anomie which accompany deviance may therefore be expected to be experienced by converts. In fact, one may suggest that feelings of anomie were a factor contributing to their conversion decision, which helps explain how disappointed they may feel when their anomic feelings continue or even grow stronger. Second, when they broke one of the greatest taboos of their community, that against apostasy, they rejected the social norms and arrangements which provided their lives with some stability, and they may no longer know what is expected. Their act of making their own choice leads to uncertainty.[1]

However, in analysing the narratives of the participants in this study, I found an additional source of feelings which may be characterised as anomie. When people make a decision to follow a new faith, they make that decision with high hopes for their possibilities and the expectation that this will give them fully realised lives, as well as for many a sense of relief that after a long time of thinking and studying, they have finally decided. This joy and relief is followed not by a life of fulfilment, but by a series of identity and community challenges. One woman recounted to me how she felt after finally deciding to adopt a Christian faith, following many months of angst-filled study and consideration: "I actually heard music and could tell there was a wedding party going on in heaven, as my name was being written in the book of life! I was so happy, I felt like I was flying after that. I finally was a daughter of God." She was so excited that she wanted to tell everyone about her decision, but she quickly realised that her enthusiasm was not shared by many others. The Christians she knew began giving her confusing instructions, and meanwhile she grew fearful of reprisals among her Muslim friends and family, so her own excitement was quickly dampered.[2]

Many participants reported going through a long list of anomic challenges as they adjusted to their new identity. Their initial enthusiasm about their change is dimmed as they realise that the path they have chosen involves its own set of not inconsiderable challenges. They find that, as is characteristic of deviants,

---

[1] See Rose 1966:31, Berger 1981:34, for explanations of this in earlier studies of deviance and anomie

[2] Ebaugh described a similar trajectory among nuns who leave the convent (Ebaugh 1988). A decision to leave was usually finalised by an external announcement, but an ex-nun then faced the process of re-defining her place in the community and found that separating herself from her identity as a nun and developing a new identity was a struggle. She also found herself trying to adjust to her new-found independence, working through broken relationships with those left behind and developing a new set of relationships. As she did this, at first she wanted to tell everyone about her change, but then started to prefer to hide her previous identity, working toward finding a way to let it come up in conversation in a natural and appropriate way.

their values are no longer exactly the same as those of their group, nor are they quite the values of Christians. They have lost the sense of moral integration which Islam and *tawhid* had provided them, and by which they had lived, or been expected to live, before converting. They also lost the structure and routine that membership in the *umma* provided.[3] They have a sense of being stuck between two worlds, wanting the best of both but finding themselves with the best of neither.

While one of the great appeals to many considering Christianity was the freedom it gave to its adherents to live their lives according to their own conscience, without Islam or their community dictating their lives, once individuals convert they realise that that strong community provided them with a dependability, a predictability, that they now miss. For example, a few people told me that they miss participating in Muslim holidays. One man said he prefers the personal, family-based nature of the Muslim holidays, and wishes he saw the same energy and communal enthusiasm for the Christian holidays. A few participants reported that the Muslim holidays are the hardest seasons of the year: the occasions no longer hold any meaning to them, but they still do have a sense that those festivals should be important and spent with family.

Loneliness is a problem for many participants. They avoid spending much time with their Muslim families, especially if they have children who they want to protect from Muslim influences. It is often dangerous to associate very much with foreigners, and Arab Christians rarely want to spend time with them. In most Arab communities, social ties are family ties, and so by weakening family ties, people are left without the social support they used to have, and they find it very hard to find a replacement social structure. This is actually increasingly symptomatic throughout much of Arab society, not specific to religious converts. As people move from their villages to cities where they are relatively anonymous, they face extreme loneliness and feel the loss of structure. These emotions can accompany or cause strong feelings of anomie.

Interestingly, studies on people converting to Islam in the West report that, coming from a very liberal society, one of the greatest appeals of Islam to them is the discipline, tight ritual structure, and the supportive community they find in fellow Muslims (Allievi 2002:1, Haddad 2006:38). However, they too can face similar feelings of anomie when they realise that the cohesiveness and structure that so attracted them are often more a function of cultural Islam than of their beliefs, and so they have to work to adapt their new faith to their culture and, in a sense, create the ideal that was missing (Haddad 2006:38, Roald 2006:65).

---

[3] See Shoham 1976:57, Rothbaum 1988:205, Stark and Bainbridge 1996:19, Cao et al 2010:626 for further discussion of the relationship between social structure and anomie

Disappointment

Idealism is a characteristic of many religious converts, and it is as idealistic desires and ambitions are not achieved that people settle into a sense of anomie. When people join a new religious community, they have high expectations, which can lead to a great deal of discontent when the new group fails to deliver all that is expected (Jacobs 1989:6). Many participants in this study discussed an idealistic sort of disappointment with all kinds of Christians, including other converts, Christian-background Arabs, and missionaries. They feel like outsiders in every group, a feeling familiar to many people in a variety of contexts,[4] but which many MBBs believe is unique to their own experience as they compare their lives to what they see in their Muslim families, Christian churches and other groups where it seems that everyone fits in better than they do.

One young man had strong complaints against people in different Christian communities he joined. He said he did not trust other converts, suspecting they were only participating in the meetings or claiming to convert for personal gain. He felt that he had been hurt by Arab Christians, and that he was often neglected by foreign Christians:

> There are other problems at church. Like when the service ends [at the international church] and everyone is greeting each other but they all ignore me. Or when I am talking to some people, and someone comes up to greet them, but ignores me. To me, this is a huge insult – it's like, I'm nothing, because I'm not from Europe!... In my culture, relationships are the most important thing. I'm not welcomed in my new life. Maybe by God, but not in the church. I've been going to [an Arab] church for five years, I've been there, they know me, but still, there is nothing, no relationship. Through the church I have also attended conferences with children from poor areas. They welcome me, they love me, and I feel like I'm one of them.

He saw every slight as yet another indicator that the community of Christians would not live up to his expectations. While his strongest words were against Arab Christians, he also learned to have low expectations of foreigners, and he felt welcomed in a community of people from a lower social class than him. While in his narrative he himself expressed suspicion of other converts, he simultaneously expressed deep frustration at the suspicion Arab Christians demonstrated toward him.

Some converts therefore place their hopes on something they have never known, such as travelling to the United States or to Europe, and some young men hope to marry a woman from the West. Anomie resulting from a strong attraction to the West in the Arab world is hardly unique to converts, but the frustrations they face as outsiders in their own communities strongly exacerbate it. Meanwhile, the sense of anomie is further exacerbated by the disappointing

---

[4] See Berger 1981:35; see also the discussion of fusive identity integration in chapter 7

example they have of Western missionaries in their country. When missionaries do not prove to be all the convert is expecting, though, they get frustrated. As already discussed, the most common complaints among my research participants were criticisms of Western missionaries, but their deep disappointment is most likely due in large part to their previously high expectations.

Most people I met lived with a sense of continuous frustration, but I did not learn of any additional acts of deviance or other changes in their lives as a result of their anomie. Many of them had only converted in recent years, so it raises questions whether they will always live lives with this type of turmoil or, if not, what they might change. Some participants told me of friends who returned to Islam because they found the stress too great, and others told me of people who saw the potential for problems and decided not to change faith because of that. One young woman told me that she almost committed suicide as she dealt with family pressure, her own desire for freedom, and the challenges she faced in living out her new life. Another woman who had converted a decade previously, told me that she is not happy, but she also said that she feels power because of her faith, and that is how she continues living.

A Perfect Believer

The participants in this study placed high value on finding new communities, but they reported great frustrations as they sought to form or join groups. Most Arab Muslims who choose to follow a Christian faith come from a religio-social context where communal commitment is expected. After converting, they try to identify both with Muslims and with Christians, and indeed social relationships play an essential role in helping them as they develop their new lives as religious changers. It is vitally important to religious converts in the Middle East that they find a new community with which they relate, and many report difficulties in learning how to relate with other converts and with born Christians.

One of the primary characteristics that many converts are looking for, is *tawhid*. They are looking for complete unity and cohesiveness among the Christians they meet, and are expecting to develop such a sense of unity with other believers, whether they join Christian communities or gather with others from a Muslim background. Many participants in this study told me that theological inclinations, culture or other constraints were not as important to them as a commitment to unity. One woman stated that she tries to avoid any exposure to controversial theological perspectives in her community because she does not want to risk bringing division to the small group of her fellow converts. Young communities of converts, in particular, are determined, even desperate, to do what it takes to maintain a sense of unity.

In this vein, many participants were highly accepting of the diversity among Christians, again in the name of unity, and were sympathetic to a number of different theological bents. When they were critical of other denominations, it was because they believed that those denominations are sectarian in nature, contributing to division through their beliefs rather than to unity. It bears mentioning, though, that few adherents to a Christian faith from a Muslim background have had much opportunity to engage with a variety of different Christian traditions, and so such theological openness is relatively easy to maintain.

Religious community is more than just a gathering of like-minded people. It is their family, it is the place where they are looking for love and acceptance, and they are well aware that other converts who join are looking for the same things. It is a place where their new identities can be developed and reinforced: people who have close contact with other converts, especially, find that their own understanding of who they are in their new faith is clarified as they spend time with others who have shared their experience.

As new followers of a Christian faith, converts are seeking to be inherently good people, living their lives to demonstrate characteristics that will help affirm the perceived rightness of their chosen faith. To understand how converts from a Muslim background define good character, it is helpful to consider their choices from a framework of honour, which is highly valued in most Arab communities. Honour is rooted in reputation or respect, and self-respect. To be honourable is to be sure that one has acted according to one's group's idea of honour, and to have the group's recognition that s/he is a valuable member (deSilva 2000:25). This respect can be conferred, usually by being born into an honourable lineage, but it is developed or strengthened through virtuous behaviour that builds up one's and one's group's reputation. Because the point of honour is the group, one of the most important virtues of an honourable person may be loyalty (McIlroy 2005:2).

Honour is determined according to image in the eyes of others.[1] A man's honour, especially, is based in his image as someone who is honest, keeps his commitments, fights against injustice, and works to further his and his family's interests. Converts desire to be inherently good people and, in their communities, what they believe is not as cogent an issue as how they live what they believe. They want to portray revered ideals such as sacrifice, loyalty, humility, love and acceptance in their own character, because that is what a good person would do – and surely, they believe, an adherent of a Christian faith should be a good person.

Relating to Fellow Believers[2]

Group membership, especially membership in a minority group, has often been found to reinforce self-esteem and strengthen one's sense of identity. Members of disadvantaged groups often desire strongly to be a part of a group, but a group that is distinct from others. "People feel better about themselves if they believe their group is different from other groups in ways that demonstrate their group is the best" (Spinner Halev and Theiss-Morse 2003:519). This perspective suggests that converts will benefit a great deal from having regular contact with other converts, in terms of self-confidence and identity formation. Though my research sample did not lend any conclusions as to whether this is true, almost every participant in this study said that this companionship of people "like them" is something they greatly desire.

[1] Anthropological studies of the Middle East throughout the 20th century identified similar community characteristics and expectations. See, for example: Zeid 1965, Moughrabi 1978.

[2] Parts of this section were published in Kraft, Kathryn: "Faith is Lived out in Community: Questions of New Community for Arab Muslims who have Embraced a Christian Faith" in St. Francis Magazine 6(6), December 2010

Most fellowship groups I met had both convert and born Christian members. Those groups that were comprised primarily of converts were new groups: few of their members had converted more than a year or two earlier. In fact, it is somewhat rare for converts to have close contact with others like them, much like other deviant groups who are unlikely to have much contact with each other (Downes and Rock 2003:26). After all, religious deviants are careful to control who knows what about their change, and associations with other deviants may potentially be problematic.

In addition to trust issues, there are often practical obstacles to developing community with other converts. For example, one woman lived on the ground floor of her building and her door was open to the neighbourhood, so she did not feel comfortable hosting Christians or faith-related meetings in her home. While she would like to take initiative in building community, she felt dependent on others' interest and availability. Another couple told me that their group of converts always met in the home of missionaries for several years, because all the converts were single and living with their families. Since their families were not interested in Christianity, it was not practicable to hold Bible studies or Christian meetings in their homes. As groups grow and as converts marry, such obstacles do begin to fade.

A different set of challenges emerges as the number of converts in a region grows and the group also grows. Increased size in a group often inevitably means that some degree of anonymity develops, since not every member can know each other member well. This can be damaging to the unity of the group and can also decrease individual members' enthusiasm and commitment levels. One man told me of how he watched the number of believers from a Muslim background in his region increase from almost none to a group too large to keep together. He mourned the unity that has been lost, saying, "Now there are lots of different groups and each group has its own ideas about things. I know this is because there are more of us now, and it is safer, but it's also because we have divided into groups where we feel more comfortable." While he is glad to see the numbers of people "like him" increasing, he yearns for a way to know each of the other converts intimately, and so to restore some unity.

Even when groups become differentiated and diffuse, there are still benefits to regular contact with other converts, to talk through their experiences, share a sense of what they left behind and the frustrations that they feel, and consider what aspects of the adopted religion they will make their own and how (Rothbaum 1988:217, Roald 2006:50). Such groups help people as they take the time they need to place distance between themselves and their pasts, to evaluate their change and begin to adjust and develop opinions about a number of different issues from a new faith lens.

On the other hand, support groups of leavers can also sometimes foster bitterness. Communities of converts out of Islam often help each other a great deal in processing their pasts and their change, but sometimes they also can become a setting in which anger and fierce attitudes against Islam and unappreciative Christian groups may grow.

Access to experienced converts who can share about their experiences and give advice to newer converts is helpful to this process. "The 'new' converts jump directly into the 'old' converts' cultural sphere and internalize convert reconceptualizations directly, without having to go through the culturalization process" (Roald 2006:52). Such a support from older converts is extremely helpful for new converts out of Islam as they attempt to work out their new identities. Particularly, they are able to avoid imprudent adaptations to Arab Christian culture that they later on decide are not necessary to their faith, such as eating pork or praying certain ritual prayers. Relationships with other converts also help them think through their own stories as they develop their own personal narratives of change, and they help young converts learn how to defend their new faith cleverly but prudently.

There is an assumed hierarchy of respect among many MBBs. This hierarchy reflects the social hierarchy of many Arab communities: according to gender and age. Women are likely to defer to the leadership of men, and a convert who is older by age assumes the respect of a younger convert, often regardless of who has been a Christian believer for longer. One woman who had been a convert for about ten years and was in her mid-forties told me about a young convert girl she had recently met. The girl was from her hometown, and was only 20 years old, but had already believed in a Christian faith for five years. The older woman told me that as soon as she met her, she sat down with the younger woman and told her that she should not confront her family because that would only cause problems in the house and was not necessary. She admonished the younger lady to be patient. As the older woman told me this, she indicated that as soon as she met the younger woman she saw her as someone who needed her mentoring and so, regardless of what the younger woman's actual needs might be, she took it upon herself to give advice. From younger converts who have been mentored and advised by older converts, I never heard a complaint about such treatment; instead, several wished they had been more cared for by older believers, converts or not.

One risk of developing strong bonds of unity among converts is that there is a strong potential for an in-group bias to result. While belonging to a group of similar people helps build self-esteem and a stronger sense of belonging, it can also lead members of the group to fail to acknowledge criticism, and to see one's group as superior to other groups, especially groups perceived as dominant, most notably Arab Christians. Some participants, especially those who were at the forefront of efforts to gather converts together, demonstrated such a tendency.

Most people from a Muslim background who choose to embrace a Christian faith, even those who find strong *umma* with other converts, still desire a connection with the historical religion of Christianity. When they make their decision, they turn first to the church. They look to Christians as role models of what they have chosen to become, and yearn to be embraced into a unified Christian community.

Most participants sought out a relationship with a church, but many also expressed deep frustration with the church. French priest Jean-Marie Gaudeul documented similar frustrations among the Muslim-background converts in his research. He found that many MBBs were not welcomed into churches and that churches often deliberately delayed granting baptism to converts from Islam. He suggested that this was largely due to church members' fear of repercussions, a sense of a history of antipathy between Christians and Muslims, and mistrust of Muslims (Gaudeul 1999:268-270). Nonetheless, he found that Christian community was essential to helping a convert in the process of changing, understanding his/her conversion and developing a theology by which to live (Gaudeul 1999:245).

When Christians do welcome Muslim-background converts into their communities, the converts may grow frustrated because they feel like the Christians are imposing much of their culture and teaching the converts to be more like them, the "authentic" Christians.[3] One woman told me that after she had made her decision, which for her was connected to the sense of freedom that she sensed in Christian doctrine, she told some Christian co-workers about her change. Their response was to give her a written prayer to Mary, telling her she should read it before going to sleep at night. She was uncomfortable with the idea of praying to Mary, and extremely frustrated because it seemed to her that she had left a religion of rules for another set of rules. This led her to question her decision, but she decided to carry on after later speaking with another Christian who affirmed her desire to live her new faith according to her conscience and her own sense of what God wanted.

A sociological theory called Symbolic Interactionism suggests that sometimes outsiders in a group may try very hard to do whatever is needed in order to be accepted by the church group because, as people seek to play a role well and are confirmed in their performance by members of the in-group, there is increased trust and commitment to the relationship, and a sense of belonging in the group (McCall and Simmons 1978, Barker and Currie 1985, Burke and Stets 1999,2009). The converse is seen in situations where people do not feel trusted by members of the in-group. For example, a young man who was disappointed by Christians, because no Christian family would consent to allowing him to marry their daughters, feels like an outsider among born Christians. Instead of establishing trust, interactions like these reinforce mutual suspicion between born Christians and Muslim-background converts, so the young man decides that he prefers not to spend time with Arab Christians at all.

To some extent, converts find they need to prove themselves to churches before they will be taken seriously. A number of participants told of visiting

[3] Converts to Islam have experienced a similar reception by born Muslims in various contexts. See, for example, Bourque 2006.

different churches, sometimes literally knocking on doors, looking for someone who would be willing to baptise them. The few churches that would even consider baptising a Muslim were looking first to receive assurances that the person was sincere about his/her conversion, but even converts who had eventually succeeded in building a relationship with a church still felt like Arab churches keep them at arm's length. While the symbolic interactionist theory about building trust might hold up to some extent, the emotional distance that Christian-born church members maintain from their Muslim-born co-religionists may never be completely surpassed, even by those converts who continue to actively interact with Christians.

The segregation may then come full-circle. Converts are relegated to finding community only with other converts, which is to their advantage, considering the aforementioned benefits that come with spending time with others "like them". As converts grow in their numbers and their understanding of their new faith, Arab Christians are more likely to be willing to welcome them in, but by then the converts have allowed an in-group bias to take root. They see themselves as following a less culturally-tainted devotion to Christ, and they already have their own groups. For example, one convert told me that a group of born Christians was hesitant to collaborate on a project with his group of converts, apparently because of a lack of trust. So, he said, he and his MBB friends would simply do their own ministry, which would be more effective since they understood Muslim culture better.[4]

As a result of all of these desires and pressures, different participants developed different expectations of how they would recreate their lives as believers in Christ. Often, their dream is not just for themselves but for a large yet unified community of Muslim-background followers of a Christian faith. They want to stand apart from the dominant majority, building a movement that will reinforce their own sense of who they are, attract new converts, and validate the MBB community (Smith and Fetner 2007:14). One participant, for example, told me that his goal was to develop a new group identity, with their own heritage and traditions. He was attending a Christian music school so that he could start building a unique cultural heritage for people from a Muslim background through musical expression. Another participant said that he sees the community of converts as currently a small, weak group within Christianity, but that they should seek to be something bigger. Instead of developing a distinct minority identity among Christians, he wants to see MBBs play a role alongside the Christian-background church, which should also be a distinct group within the larger realm of Christianity.

It bears mention that a few participants emphasised that, if legal barriers against conversion did not exist, then they would not have to weigh such concerns so heavily. Since Christianity and Islam are presently legislated civil statuses, converts find themselves feeling the need to fit into a category, but

---

[4] For parallels to the experience of converts to Islam, see Roald 2006.

preferring to focus on their beliefs rather than on their community. They prefer to associate with the "global church" of people who share their doctrinal beliefs in the world, regardless of culture or ethnicity.

So it is that many participants have avoided affiliating with a Christian church. Irregardless of the cold welcome many felt when they first visited, they believe that apostasising from their born religion was an act of freedom and that is a freedom they can only continue to exert if they do not ascribe to any label or institution. While they would affirm that they share the same beliefs with most practising Christians in their country, they see themselves as privileged that they do not have to fit into the label of the ethnic Christian minority. The perfect believer, for them, is a person of character and faith, not a person with a label.

Relating to the Community of One's Birth

As a new believer in a Christian faith, one of the most challenging concerns is determining how best to relate to one's birth community. Converts usually wish to respect their families and demonstrate that they are still good and honourable people, but they also wish to be loyal to their own consciences within their new belief system. While theories on honour and shame in society are considered by many scholars to be outdated, the perspective of these theories resonates strongly with the values and experiences of participants in this study. They understand that their communities live according to these values, and so they themselves continue to adhere to them. While indeed many factors are at play in addition to honour, honour is nonetheless of key importance. This may be more true for converts than for other citizens, since they want to present a good image of who they are in their new identity. Pierre Bourdieu reflected that an honour-based sentiment is mostly found in societies where relationships with others take precedence over relationships with oneself (Bourdieu 1965:212). While this may or may not be true about converts, most of them are eager that they at least continue to demonstrate a respect for the community, both for their own reputation and for the good of the community.

A family, village or other society of people is the primary audience of a person's behaviour. For someone who lives in a community that places great value on honour, what is expected and permitted should be understood perfectly. In describing a North African Berber community several decades ago, Bourdieu quoted Montesquieu to summarise how behaviour is regulated in a community according to honour: "What is forbidden by honour is even more forbidden when the laws do not forbid it; and what honour prescribes, is even more obligatory when the laws do not demand it" (in Bourdieu 1965:230). This is because honourable acts are performed out of respect for the collectivity. Motivation is high to do that which will bring honour not only to oneself but also to the family, tribe, society, and religious community, and by the same token avoid doing what would bring dishonour, or shame (Baker 2003:24).

There is in many families an unspoken code of rules that insiders know or are expected to know: they are aware of their duties and their place in their kin structure, village and community and they would be lost if separated from the system (Peristiany 1965). Based on this, they decide what to do and what to tell whom. Though honourable behaviour is often recognisable outside of the group, each group has its own idea of what specifically is honourable (deSilva 2000:25). Converts leaving the religion of their community may feel they are expected to know, and expect themselves to know, their home communities' rules with reference to how people will react to their apostasy, but this is not always the case.

Especially when apostates fled their homes years, or even decades, ago, they may not always fully understand anymore. After all, even though the values of honour and shame are deeply rooted in Arab society, all communities are dynamic and may change. Even so, it is important to them that they have a sense that they know, because that innate ability to function within their communities' honour/shame paradigm is what roots them as members of the community. Individuals will generally convince themselves that they understand their communities perfectly well. Their identity as a member of their community is based on their knowledge of its code of honour: if an individual doubts that s/he knows his/her own family, s/he will likely feel particularly insecure.

The other side of honour is shame. When honour is bestowed, shame is removed; when honour is tainted, shame is what results. One's honour is often strengthened or restored when another is shamed. Shame is often perceived as the result of behaviour that is against the group's values, such as putting one's own well-being above that of the community. Many families will go to great lengths to avoid being shamed, which is the principle behind many honour killings: a family restores its honour when an adulterous sister or daughter is killed, thereby eliminating her shame. When there is a perceived stain on a woman's honour, the family will often seek to eliminate the damage she has done, which may mean eliminating her (Dodd 1973:42, McIlroy 2005:2). This is especially likely if honour is already fragile. The same principle lies behind attempts to remove the shame of a family member's apostasy (Slaughter 1993:197). While apostates are rarely known to be killed in the Arab world, it is frequently considered and threatened. One participant in this study gave me a detailed account of how his mother's brothers kept him tied up in an abandoned building for more than two months, sometimes beating him, almost starving him, and bringing in religious leaders to try to convince him to choose Islam over Christianity. His uncles did this to avoid their nephew's apostasy, and they did it in a remote location in an attempt to preserve the family's honour throughout the process.

Another way to diminish shame is to pass blame as far from themselves as possible. Often, families will choose to blame their relative's apostasy on the influence of a non-family member. This happens most frequently for women, whose husbands make a likely target. According to Arab partrilineality, though a woman is responsible to her husband, she keeps her family name, and her honour is tied up in that of her birth family. One woman, who converted several months after husband, told me that when she informed her family of her decision, her family sent her nice gifts with Qur'anic verses in an attempt to attract her back to Islam. When she insisted that she was committed to her Christian identity, they blamed her husband and told her that her faith is not her own fault.

One of the main issues affected by this concern for how the community will perceive and understand certain behaviours, is the question of who knows what about a changed faith. Most known converts and people who work with believers of a Muslim background see this as a problem that needs to be overcome in order for people to follow Christ, or Christianity, in the way they would want. They are looking for a society and a time when people will be able to change faith not only in their own consciousness, but in public as well. The fact that conversion to a Christian faith is deviant in most of their communities, means that many keep their faith a secret, experiencing stunted emotional development, limited opportunities for religious instruction, and other challenges. Many people make their decisions based more on the expectations of family or the larger community, and less on what they may think is best for themselves as individuals. To do otherwise, particularly when the individual decision is unlikely to reflect well in the community, may lead to conflict. It is perceived as an act of rebellion.

Striving to be the Perfect Believer but Labelled a Deviant

The decision to, and method of, "coming out", that is, making a faith change known, is one of the most significant decisions faced by a Muslim who chooses to embrace a Christian faith. After all, their apostasy is a form of social and religious deviance in their communities. People who leave Islam face disapproval or myriad other challenges as a result of that decision. Religious deviance is not an unfamiliar concept in the West: conversion to any faith system that bears a stigma may be considered religious deviance, for example conversion to New Religious Movements or Hinduism in the United States.

Discussions of deviance have centred around the concept of social control and the role it may or may not play in a society.[5] Arguably honour and shame

[5] Deviance has come and gone in sociological investigation. Some theorists consider it to be too simplistic and others believe that it is no longer relevant to post-modern societies in this globalised information technology age. But in recent years it has màde a comeback, particularly in relation to the concept of anomie. Recent theories have explored the relationship between criminality and factors such as the urge to achieve culturally-defined goals, commitment to staying within the bounds of what is considered culturally legitimate, and monetary dissatisfaction (Baumer and Gustafson 2007, Cao et al 2010, Baron 2011). The exploration of deviance here is less concerned with causes of

dynamics are a form of social control, but ultimately the forces defining what is and is not socially acceptable are internalised and become a part of an individual's own values. Affective family ties are deeply valued by most of the converts I have met. As such, rather than responding out of fearful submission to control, it is as often as not their preference to build their family's honour and maintain strong ties. Nonetheless, the very word "Islam" means submission. Strong social expectations are found in most Arab communities of the Middle East, so it may be that most people who would otherwise be inclined to stop submitting, will not stop. The few who do become deviant.

As people are being exposed to a variety of ideas, though, more and more will choose to pursue those deviant options. Erving Goffman's classic book *Stigma* still provides some of the best insight into how deviants are perceived by, and interact with, those around them. *Stigma*, like much of the literature on deviance, was written for a Western, usually American, audience, but it provides some interesting insights into the lives of converts to a Christian faith in Muslim society. Goffman distinguishes between the "discredited" and the "discreditable". The discredited have a stigma that is known to the community, often as soon as someone sees them – for example, a marked physical handicap. The discreditable, on the other hand, have a secret which, if known, would stigmatise them in society. Deviants fit the discreditable category if they are able to hide their deviancy; once their deviancy is known (i.e. when labelling happens), they too will become discredited (Goffman 1963:57).

While theories about honour and shame may be frequently used to define social control structures in Middle Eastern society but rarely applied to Western society, similar principles do apply in communities around the world. There are some especially useful parallels with literature on homosexuality as a similar type of stigma. Homosexuality presents an interesting comparison because, like apostasy, there are some who strongly support it but there are many who believe it is either wrong, or not necessary. In American evangelical circles, conversion from Islam to Christianity is heralded, while homosexuality is taken as rejection. In European academic circles, there is often a great deal of sympathy for homosexuality, but little patience for conversion to Christianity. As it happens, in Arab Muslim communities, both are usually acts of deviance.

Sexually stigmatised people may conceal their orientations because of a feeling of shame and guilt about who they feel they are, knowing that their "coming out" has the potential to cause problems for the people they love. Also, having been raised in a society which sees their new identity as deviance, they feel guilt. Such emotions are a large part of why they hesitate to disclose, but concealment is not easy.

---

deviance, returning instead to an older model focusing on the stigma that comes with deviance, and how certain types of stigma can result from various types of deviation from societal norms.

Many of the converts I met lived with a degree of dualism, but it was difficult for them to enjoy simple and relaxed relationships. A stigmatised person, particularly one who remains discreditable, can experience a high level of stress. It takes psychological effort to hold back feelings and thoughts, and there has been extensive psychological research demonstrating that the stress in keeping a stigmatising secret affects both mental and physical health among people who may be sexually stigmatised (DiPlacido 1998:148, Bybee et al 2009:144). This stress and personal management becomes an intrinsic part of the individual's identity: because a stigmatised person grows accustomed to dealing with these situations, s/he may become quite skilled at managing them (Goffman 1963:31).

It is also more difficult for discreditable people to access channels of support from other gays or sympathetic supporters (Bybee et al 2009:145). Furthermore, it is not always easy to put a label on deviance. Many converts know that they have experienced a change in their beliefs and possibly even in their sense of religious loyalty, but they do not know exactly how to define this. Until they have a firm sense of who they are, it is difficult for them to express this clearly to others.

As the outsider researcher, I was often privy to selective information, because discreditable people considered me "wise". Similarly, among gay and bisexual men, it is common to come out to friends before family, and they may or may not wait even longer to make their stigma publicly known. "Each setting and relationship contains a chance of rejection and/or vitimization, and each therefore requires an independent decision about disclosure" (Hill 2009:353). Deciding how and when to come out to parents is often the most complicated and belaboured of decisions (Carnelley et al 2011). It is likely that intimate people will be put off as much as, or even more than, strangers by a stigma; therefore, it is often most important to hide one's discrediting characteristic from close relations (Goffman 1963:65).

"A very widely employed strategy of the discreditable person is to handle his risks by dividing the world into a large group to whom he tells nothing, and a small group to whom he tells all and upon whose help he then relies" (Goffman 1963:117). Often this small group consists of people who share the same stigma, but not necessarily. This will depend on the perceived risks of trusting others who come from the same background, regardless of whether they share a stigma. Many of the participants in this study spoke of different circles of relationships they had. These circles were defined according to trust. Even though I first met many of the participants on the day of the interview, I was immediately welcomed into an innermost circle because I was a foreigner and not related to the community where they might be discredited. I also came recommended by mutual friends in this inner circle. Friends and acquaintances may know that the convert thinks differently, but may not know the full extent of their differences. Families are often on the outermost circle, because their reaction to the stigma will be the most personal.

Whether a person is discredited or discreditable has a large effect on his/her life. To make the choice to self-disclose, to go from being discreditable to discredited, particularly to one's parents, makes it possible to start taking adaptive actions. Research has found that coming out as gay is likely to lead to better psychological health, a stronger gay solidarity movement, and the ability to live in community with other gays. On the other hand, there is a recognised risk of lost friends, family or employment (Armstrong (E.) 2002, Hill 2009, Carnelly et al 2011). Bybee et al suggest that there are various types and means of disclosure, concluding that those who come out in such a way that they are able to integrate their identity into their wider community experience decreased shame, guilt and depression. Those who come out with pride and anger continue to experience the emotional fall-out of their deviant identity (Bybee et al 2009).

In other words, coming out on one's own terms, with a carefully thought-out sensitivity to the pressures of the community, is extremely important to the discreditable. The emphasis placed on "coming out" tends to portray disclosure as a sign of maturity, but too easily ignores the risk involved (Hill 2009:349). These findings from research with sexually stigmatised groups resonate well with the narratives of converts in the Middle East. While careful management of knowledge about a deviant identity is important to the convert's own mental health and also to his/her prospects of successfully re-integrating into community life, the choice does not always exist. Others may find out, whether or not the individual chooses to self-disclose. Sometimes someone is labelled as deviant even before s/he has made a conscious decision to pursue a deviant path. Or, if they have changed their beliefs but not yet worked out how that affects their identity, they may find that others define it for them, often ascribing them with a greater degree of deviance than they themselves may desire.

Indeed, while secret deviance is in many ways not deviance at all, sometimes converts are stigmatised by their families because of a demonstrated interest in something Christian, even before even they decide if they want to change beliefs. Their parents or brothers may start taking action against their conversion in a proactive attempt to avoid shame, before they are even seriously considering a change. In such cases, while family pressure may have convinced them to keep their religious interests to themselves, it also pushed them to more seriously consider studying that which piqued their interest. One young woman told me that her teacher saw her with a Bible before she had spent much energy exploring it, and reprimanded her then told her parents that she was considering converting, so her parents started to argue with her and limit her movement. In response, she hid her Bible but was more curious than ever. She eventually decided to make a faith decision: she grew into the deviant label that was assigned to her.

Although her relationship with her parents continued to be strained and marked with suspicion, she did not tell her family about her decision.

Therefore, even though she became deviant, she was still discreditable in their eyes. As long as she does not openly declare apostasy, her family can maintain its honour in their community and hope that she will continue to be a good daughter until she is married and out of the home. She also continues to maintain some control over the flow of knowledge about her own beliefs, which helps her to manage her stigma.

A Believer Honouring the Family? Don't Ask Don't Tell

The young woman's family allowed her the space to maintain a certain ambivalence. Her situation illustrated a common solution to stigma management, which many converts I met used effectively. They came from strongly cohesive families and they desired to maintain their commitment to the honour of their family; after all, what an individual does is projected onto his/her family by other members of the community. Shame is a truly powerful force in keeping families unified. So, because an individual is likely to feel shame on behalf of, or because of, the actions of his/her kin or close relations, there is a strong sense of responsibility to each other: affective ties within tight-knit groups, especially families, are particularly strong. In short, converts know that their loyalty to the group and its honour is assumed, and often do not want their new faith to necessarily be about shaming the family.

Conversely, Muslim families generally feel a strong affection for the deviant member of the family, as well as a need to erase the shame of having a deviant member. Some families seem to be much more concerned with erasing the shame, even at the expense of the well-being of their own loved one, and a few accept the shame out of affection for the deviant family member. Many families choose to simply ignore a shameful choice. Adapting terminology from debates on homosexuality, they adopt a policy of Don't Ask Don't Tell, particularly in their closest family relationships.

Families often ignore signs of change, or ask the deviant to refrain from flaunting his/her new identity. A number of participants assured me that their families did not know about their change, even if they were clearly acting like Christians. Such individuals may regularly go out on Sunday mornings, have left their home or country for a time, or have at least adopted some words into their vocabulary that are associated with Christian Arabs. Such changes are indicators that there was a deeper change of some sort in their lives, but their families do not question them about it. Is their family really that ignorant, or does their family make an effort not to notice, or is it important to the individual to think that his/her family does not know?

One interviewee insisted that his family does not know about his faith, even though his brother once saw him go to church and his father then confronted him about it, kicking him out of the house. Two weeks after that his brother met with him and asked him to come back to live at home but not go to church anymore. He agreed and returned home, but continued to attend church every

Sunday morning and spend much of his free time with Christians. I questioned him how it could be that he was living an overtly Christian lifestyle and yet his family no longer suspected anything. He told me that his family probably chose not to suspect: "Either they expect me to be conforming to the family's desires, or my father's just not saying anything. My mum will sometimes say on Sunday morning, don't come back too late! But we don't talk about it to avoid arguing."

In many situations it seems as if the convert him/herself is eager to believe that his/her family does not see anything. One convert took me and some other Christian friends to meet his extended family and warned us to use his Muslim name and not refer to anything that would give away his Christian identity. Though we agreed, throughout the visit we accidentally used his Christian name and referred to things about his life such that, if his family had been at all interested in confronting an apparent change in his life, we gave them plenty of evidence. Yet no one commented on it. Perhaps more importantly, the convert himself believed that this part of his extended family was unaware that he had changed faiths.

Many participants assured me that their honour in the community is secure, at least until they or someone else chooses to reveal their apostasy. This is the unspoken rule of an honour-based society. When someone commits a shameful act, as long as it remains hidden on the surface, the perpetrator can pretend s/he did not commit it, and the community can pretend they did not see it, then life can continue as normal. Don't Ask, Don't Tell.

When it is openly exposed, though, those closest to the apostate can no longer ignore it. This is why there are also stories of people being beaten by their fathers or brothers, or, less frequently, of honour killings which are most likely to be carried out by a discredited woman's brother.

While it does require facing the ongoing stresses of the life of the discreditable, Don't Ask Don't Tell is not difficult to achieve in many families because, as many participants explained to me, it is absolutely unthinkable to their families that they might become Christian. After all, most Muslims are fiercely committed to *tawhid* of the *umma* and to the honour of their community. They believe that Islam is the culmination of religions and that Muhammad is the last of the Prophets, and legal conversion is simply impossible in most Arab countries. Several said that in their own conversion process, the possibility of religious change was not something they considered until quite late in their spiritual journey. One woman explained: "It is just unthinkable for my family that someone would leave Islam, completely something they can't conceive. So they never really believed it. For me, it was a process to start to think that I might change."

When converts' families have no sense of possibility of change, they may feel more freedom in living their lives as followers of Christianity. For the sake of family cohesiveness, certain things are never mentioned, such as that the individual might have become a Christian. However, much about his/her change is said openly. They might discuss changed values, changed practices, changed language, and Christian friends. The deviance that an actual conversion would be, however, is not acknowledged. Some people even go so far as to tell their families about their change, but avoiding statements that would be offensive. One woman, for example, told her family that she met a Christian family and that they were good people and that she became "like them." She told me that it would have been too difficult to actually come out and say that she'd become a Christian, but she was sure that her family knew what she meant. Her family now knows exactly who their sister/daughter is, but has chosen to ignore the shame that a conversion to Christianity would bring by refusing to put a name on it.

Several still-discreditable participants had stories of spirited religious dialogue they had exchanged with their parents or siblings in which their family argued the side of Islam and they represented the message from the Gospels. When this was not done in a confrontational way, it seems to have been mutually appreciated and enjoyed within the family. Several people did tell me that when they first converted they had been very confrontational with their families, criticising the Qur'an and Muslim practices, but as they matured they realised that it was better for them to pursue peace in their homes. They told me that, in some ways, a degree of deceit, or at least a careful approach such as evading questions, shows more love and respect for their parents than confronting them with a harsh truth.

Demonstrating the Character of a Good Believer

While Don't Ask Don't Tell is helpful for maintaining community and honour, some degree of public declaration is an important phase in many people's conversion process. It is the point of no return, and it is also many Christian believers' understanding of scripture that they can only be true believers if they confess their faith and do not deny God. Some participants actually reported that they had not themselves been sure of what they believed before they found themselves declaring it openly. The moment of declaration was the moment they knew what they had chosen for themselves. There are many ways of doing this, however, and different audiences for such a confession.

Baptism is a Christian sacrament which can serve the purpose of being an open declaration of a new faith. Some converts believe that baptism is essential for them to complete the process of conversion, while for others it is merely an opportunity to publicly declare what they believe. As such, the invitation list for a baptism is a very important consideration for many converts. Who they will discredit themselves to and when, often hinges on who witnesses their baptism.

Almost all participants in this study had been baptised when I met them, but for many their baptism was in private with only a few trusted people present. Even some who thought their faith identity as "followers of Christ" did not affect their ethnic identity as Muslims at all, felt that it was important to be baptised even though that ritual is so closely affiliated with Christianity as an institutional religion. Some converts are reticent to consider being baptised because of this association, but most usually come to see it as a symbol of their faith. Their baptism may be in a church, or a river, or a bathtub, depending on who they want to witness it and how they want the witnesses to interpret the event. Participation in other Christian rituals can also be a form of declaration, for example participation in the Eucharist or even, in some cases, the decision to marry a Christian.

This discussion builds on the understanding that most converts desire to honour their communities and respect the values of their families. This was indeed an underlying theme throughout the narratives of my research. While converts want to exert their own individual consciences, in some cases even in a spirit of rebellion, most still desire to remain connected to their own culture. Those values continue to be deeply embedded in how they make day-to-day decisions. In fact, many, since they know that their decision can bring shame on their home communities, are particularly determined to act honourably in other ways.

On the other hand, as they learn about Christ and Christianity, they are often exposed to a theology that teaches them to exalt shame. Some scholars have argued that Jesus and St. Paul taught people to not care about the world's ideas of honour and shame, and in fact that Christ's shameful death was to be an example to Christians of how to shun honour in the eyes of men, even though Jesus himself lived in a strong honour/shame-based society (deSilva 1994:439,441). The early centuries of Christian history tell a story of a religion that grew through the willingness of its members to be shamed in society (deSilva 1994:440, Waetjen 2001:719-720). This theological teaching seems contradictory to the culture from which Arab MBBs come, and they may feel like they are torn between two cultures rooted in two opposing theologies.

How converts change in their relationship to honour and shame, as a result of a change in belief, varies. Many continue to conform to the community's expectations of maintaining honour, at least for a time. However, some converts do in fact seem to try to go against the flow as a part of their new identity. This is a difficult tension to negotiate, and most converts go through different phases in the process of maturing in their new faith. For a while they may continue to do everything they can to keep up appearances for the sake of community honour, but then become determined to demonstrate to their family that they will not be controlled by community pressure. Eventually they may learn to create balance by respecting their family and acting honourably while remaining true to what they believe.

Though a large component of honour is maintaining the community's expectation of status quo, it is also a defining characteristic of an honourable person that s/he is visibly a good person. Therefore, if an apostate is in fact an honourable person in all other ways, especially if s/he contributes to the community in some visible and significant way, often s/he can eventually come to be accepted and even respected in the community. One participant's eldest brother was the first convert in their family. When his conversion became known, he was threatened, beaten, expelled from the community, and treated as if dead. Years later, he did something very helpful for his brother, something which was considered truly honourable, and he was welcomed back into the family and respected by his father as his most beloved son. His Christian identity even became a part of his father's boasts and his father began to refer to him affectionately as 'the priest'. It bears mentioning that this seems much more plausible for men than for women, as the pressures on women are different and usually more intense. His sisters were never received in kind by their father after they converted.

Many converts see their own success and honourable acts as something that will both be beneficial to their families and decrease the shame presently associated with conversion to Christianity. Some participants told me that their strongest evangelistic tool in attracting other Muslims to Christianity was their own success in school and/or their careers. One man told me that his responsible behaviour and his success at work made it much more difficult for his parents to reject him when he decided to tell them about his decision. It also gave him more confidence to tell them, rather bluntly, about his change. Another young man, a friend of his, was working hard at his university studies when I met him, saying he was highly motivated to find a good job upon graduating because he wanted to be an upstanding member of the community and fulfil the expectations of his family, who did not yet know about his change. This would also help him build a good name for the growing number of converts from Islam.

The dream of the perfect believer, what converts look to Arab Christians to exemplify, what they themselves aspire to be, especially among other Muslims – converted Muslims and their still-Muslim families alike – is of a good, honourable and courageous person. They believe Christians must be willing to take risks for what they believe. Don't Ask Don't Tell, and the willingness to remain discreditable, is not for them an act of cowardice. Rather, living with such a complex web of relationships and messages is burdensome and exhausting, marked by a constant sense of anxiety about potential disclosure or misunderstandings. It is out of respect both for their families and for the message of love they found in their study of Christian scriptures, that they aspire to a life of integrity before God, even if this means risk before man and a high degree of personal stress.

A Perfect Identity

Increasingly controversial in missiological circles is a discussion about the identity of people from a Muslim background who choose to follow a Christian faith. Even the phraseology of how to refer to them is problematic. I have chosen thus far to use the most controversial of all terms, convert, to refer to the group of people that has been the focus of this research, because of its basic definition as a break with something about one's past, a turning. I have used this term with the awareness that many readers of this book may deeply dislike it, but I recognise that there is no label that would please all groups. It remains that convert is the most theoretically descriptive word to use.

The issue of identity was largely what first motivated my study of this topic, but I have saved the discussion of this impassioned topic for the end, because many other issues emerged that were complex and challenging for converts in the Arab world. Actually, all of the issues discussed thus far are a part of the complicated processes of identity negotiation, and they help elucidate why the concept of identity is so dear to the hearts both of converts, and of the Christians who work with them.

In this chapter, I will summarise some identity theory that helps to conceptualise what happens in a person's sense of who they are, when they make a decision to leave the religious community in which they were raised and set off into a new faith journey. Then I discuss how those theories help illuminate what happens in Arab Muslim communities when someone makes a decision for a Christian faith or, as some prefer to say, to "follow Christ." Each convert is an individual and faces these issues in his/her own way, but there are some common themes, and some strategies employed by converts to do this with as little emotional disruption as would be appropriate, considering the very real process of "turning" that they have undergone.

My basic premise is that there is some clear basis for identifying converts as fully "Muslim" and also as fully "Christian". This is not easy to do, though, and some high emotional and personal prices are paid by converts, in large part due to their efforts to do the right thing in terms of redefining their own identities.

Some Theories of Identity

What exactly is meant by the term "identity" varies from one situation to another. It most generally refers to a sense of self and of belonging: how people know and understand themselves, as individuals, as people who play specific roles, and as members of specific groups (Cook-Huffman 2008:20).

While there is an extensive body of theory written about identity, it has been mainly developed in a Western context, focused on individuals in the United States or Europe; even so, it is a diverse body of literature with various perspectives and little by way of common themes of discussion (Schwartz et al 2011). One of the most fundamental questions regarding identity, about which there has been little agreement or dialogue across disciplines, is to what extent identity formation is individual, and to what extent identity is socially formed. The classic thinkers of Sociology, including Marx and Durkheim, emphasised the role of society over the individual, while many personality theorists of the twentieth century, led by Psychologist Eric Erikson, emphasised the individual nature of identity. More recent theories have increasingly acknowledged a degree of both social and personal interaction in identity formation, but still with little common understanding of the degree and manner in which they interact (Schwartz et al 2011:7).

Symbolic interactionism, discussed in the previous chapter, uses the concept of roles that a person plays, to provide a framework for seeing both a social and a personal element in identity. It also provides a model for how someone can simultaneously hold and maintain more than one identity, especially in a globalised context where people are balancing more and more roles at a given time (Beyer 1994, Ameli 2002). While a more traditional view of identity sees it as unaltered and fixed, the variety of interactions which accompany globalisation confirm the changeability of identity.

As different societies have increasing contact with each other, it has been suggested that it is becoming more important to people that they have a sense of the unique identity of their community, as a means of coping with challenges from outside the group and of competing on the global scale (Beyer 1994, Smith and Fetner 2007:13). This sense of identity may be referred to as collective identity, and is usually something that is ascribed to a group and its members (Mol 1978, Hammond 1988, Burke and Stets 2009:119). This is different from social identity, which is merely an individual type of identity whose main influence is interpersonal, or social, relationships. While individual (or core) identity is generally defined in terms of personality and development, and social (or relational) identity is defined in social interactions such as a person's jobs and friendships, collective identity is about the social structures and groups in which a person roots him/herself.

Group culture forms an identity which is taken for granted by most people, even though many have other elements in their sense of self not embodied in their group's culture (Cook-Huffman 2008). Collective identity is a group culture, but it is also embodied by a specified social group, with shared understandings and loyalties defining the group's priorities and values, often in a way that defies the logic of outsiders (Beyer 1994:63, Jasper 2007:90). An individual does not necessarily have a relationship with others who share a collective identity: what matters is a cognitively-based sense of belonging to a group, such as a feeling of belonging in the *umma* which may or may not be reinforced by experience (Karim 2009:9). It can be expressed through various forms of attachment, with various contents and meanings (Verkuyten 2011:35). Identity is socially constructed, and collective identity is usually defined by members of the group. Group boundaries are drawn and crystallised over time to become something that is experienced as very real by the members of the group (Cook-Huffman 2008:26).

A shared collective identity provides a foundation for loyalty to the group and fosters an expectation that members of the group can count on each other (Alexander 2000:157-158). Religion is a particularly powerful tool in defining a group to which its members have allegiance and which provides a shared identity to its adherents. It can provide a rationale for maintaining unity within a society or community and be the basis of an argument for shared values, and against individualism. Religion as a collective identity can motivate people to action or keep them unified even when there are strong pressures pulling them apart. For these reasons, collective identity is often more important to members of minority groups, or those who may feel their groups are weak. Collective identity may then be more about claiming membership in a minority group, thus strengthening the group, than about its members' beliefs or self-perceptions (Modood 1997:332).

At the same time, religious identity is not one single concept, and does not mean the same thing to everyone affiliated with a given religion. A religious affiliation might involve any or several of the following: a sense of connection with the divine, beliefs, ritual, community involvement, family, and attitude towards co-religionists in the rest of the world (Lazerwitz 1973:205-206). When someone has a strong sense of "the subjective system of 'ultimate' relevance", it defines his/her priorities and identity (Luckmann 1967:71), and since religion can provide this, it might be perceived as the most significant component of identity for many people. The search for religion is like the search for identity; in fact, the two often do express themselves simultaneously. A belief system which roots someone in the supernatural and gives a promise of something greater can give an individual sense of self and meaning that activities and philosophical suggestions cannot (Jenkins 1996:10, Verkuyten 2011:34). A religious creed can address the innermost needs of a person and therefore touch at the very essence of identity. Nonetheless, considering that identity does involve a strong personal element, it is reasonable to assume that different people place different degrees of weight on these dimensions.

Religious affiliation is not necessarily the same as collective identity. Some sociologists of religion suggest that people's sense of religion as a set of beliefs, and their sense of spirituality, are becoming more important, while collective religious identifications are decreasing in importance (Heelas and Woodhead 2005). Sometimes religion continues to be a source of collective identity, a sense that one is a part of a larger group of people who share both a history and a creed, even while direct social reinforcement of that religious identity is decreasing in importance (Davie 1994). Indeed, for many people in many places, religion continues to provide a strong basis for collective identity.

It could be argued that in societies which place great value on community cohesiveness and honour, such as where the *tawhid* of the *umma* are very important, collective identity is expected to be the main source of a person's sense of self. Identity is taken for granted, and existence and destiny are perceived and described within the community, as being stable and predictable: "An individual is born as a member of a certain family, clan and tribal system, belonging to a circle of social life that is confined within a clearly demarcated and stable social and cultural setting, and is largely unable – should it be wished – to escape from one's allotted destiny, status or situation" (Ameli 2002:91). Identity in such a society is ruled by the community's past, and there is no conscious choice required or allowed.

A collective identity does not invalidate a sense of core identity or social identity: all are essential aspects to understanding a person's sense of self. A person does not have only one way of identifying him/herself. While in Arab countries people have most tended to describe themselves in terms of collective identities (as a Muslim, a member of a given tribe, or a native of a specific village), they do also have core and social identifications. Identity is probably becoming increasingly individualised over time (Roy 2004), even though individual identity in an Arab Muslim context is still often collectively defined, for example by focusing on one's family instead of village, or one's Islamic group instead of the larger *umma*. Many people nonetheless see themselves in terms of collective identity, but they want to be able to individually choose their collective identity and how exactly they will associate to it (Modood 1997, Roy 2004). Even a highly collective society is comprised of individuals, so different individuals in the community can react to change and new inputs differently. Symbolic interactionism theory reminds us that people may manage a number of different identities and identity types in the different roles that they play in society.

In some ways, this gets to the heart of the identity crisis facing converts from Islam into a Christian faith. Most of them make a decision to change after a long and careful investigation of doctrine, choosing to reject Muslim doctrine and adopt Christian doctrine. They and their Muslim relations associate Christian doctrine with Christian religion, and thus with a collective Christian identity. Many participants told me that they themselves do not immediately make this association, but that their families assume it. However, because of their new sense of community honour and their commitment to their families, they do not want to give up their Muslim identity. They want to choose both but recognise that the history of polarisation between Islam and Christianity makes that difficult.

Why Identity Matters

Considering the dynamics of the Muslim-majority societies where the participants in this study live, most participants felt they could not fully abandon their identity as Muslims. In many countries, not only would that be blatant apostasy, but it is actually impossible to leave Islam as a legal identification. Also, although members of their society may see their faith change as an abandonment of the community, that is not usually their wish. To them, their change is a change in beliefs, not a change in culture or society.

Even though many do desire a closer connection with Western culture and Christian communities, they continue to feel a close tie and obligation to their families, and are actively seeking ways to remain in their communities without needing to abide by the faith of those around them. They find this especially challenging when out of their own sense of *tawhid*, they desire unity between the various aspects of their lives and discover how unlikely such unity is for religious changers.

The solution of some missionaries has been to suggest a high level of contextualisation of Christianity to a Muslim milieu. Many Arab converts have told me they are troubled by the suggestion that highly "contextualised" converts (participants in what has more recently been dubbed the "Insider Movement") do not consider themselves "Christian", since, as far as these Arab converts are concerned, all believers in Christ from a Muslim background have in fact adopted "Christianity", or else are theologically confused. They worry that those individuals have not experienced a full turning of the heart, which seems to necessarily entail a rejection of Islam: as mentioned in the introduction, there is little evidence that one can fully embrace a new faith without rejecting that which s/he is leaving. Their greater concern, however, is that such individuals want to adopt Christianity fully, but without the cost of the stigma that comes with a religiously deviant choice in the eyes of their society.

Considering this dynamic, among Arabs of a Muslim background who choose to follow a Christian faith, I argue that Islam becomes their ethnicity, while Christianity becomes their religion. As globalisation brings increased pluralism, stable identifications are being thrown into doubt. Thus, for people leaving Islam as a faith system, their religious identification as Muslims, which they once experienced as a stable and immutable identity, becomes less essential to who they are. When their Muslim faith is no longer immutable, it becomes susceptible to change. Among those leaving Islam and embracing "Christ", it is abandoned and replaced by a Christian faith. However, Muslim faith is still important to members of their community and rooted in their own lives, and therefore they discard the religious identity into which they were born at great social risk, and often great psychological cost as well (Hammond 1988:5).

Philip Hammond, seeking to explain the dynamics of certain immigrant communities in the United States, argued that, while religion is significant in forming ethnicity, it is only sometimes equivalent to ethnicity. He listed the Jews, Amish, Mormons and Hutterites in the United States as groups whose religious identification is their ethnic identification, but explained that that does not mean the faith behind those religions is essential to all members of those ethnic groups (Hammond 1988:3). Muslim minorities in Western countries also frequently develop a strong sense of Muslim identity, which is primarily an ethnic identity but may or may not be a strong identification with Islam as a belief system (Lewis 2002:75). Ethnic-religious identifications vary both in strength and in meaning from one individual to another.

Saied Reza Ameli similarly suggests that in Islam, a distinction could be made between Islamic identity, which is about the fundamentals of Islam (the holy books, Islamic law, etc.), and Muslim identity, which is much more encompassing and internalized in the identities of individuals. Muslim identity is defined socially, historically, politically, and psychologically (Ameli 2002:30). A person born into a Muslim family will have some sense of this Muslim identity. For many, Muslim identity may be the essence of his/her identity and may at different points in an individual's life be connected in different ways to Islamic religious identity. A person who converts into Islam adopts an Islamic identity, but may choose to adopt part or all of the society, history, politics and psychology of Muslim identity (Ameli 2002:111).

With this framework in mind, I suggest that among converts from Islam to Christianity, "Muslim" remains their ethnic identification, which they continue to experience as an immutable stable niche, but it changes significantly in meaning. When its meaning no longer involves adherence to the Islamic creed, a space is opened up for a new faith, in this case a Christian faith, which also becomes a part of their identity albeit approached as a more transient and negotiable identification. Their Muslim identity remains a strong collective identity, while Christian identity may be only a personal identity. Whether it becomes a part of a collectivity depends on how a convert associates to Christians and/or other converts.

Most participants maintained a sense of Muslim identity as defined by Ameli's formulation, but also adopted a Christian identity. Their Muslim identification may therefore be referred to as their ethnic identity, and their Christian identification as their religious identity. Hammond points out that ethnic identifications, whether or not they include a religious element, are mainly ascribed identifications, but many people adopt chosen identifications as well. He suggests that the chosen identity often becomes more important than the ascribed identity (Hammond 1988:4). Among the participants in this study, most expressed a great deal of passion for their chosen identity as Christians, while often referring to their ascribed Muslim identity as something they had to deal with and did not want to completely abandon anyway, mainly because they still love their families and their countries.

As their connection to Islam becomes merely an ethnic identification, it gradually feels less important, and their commitment to the Muslim community wanes. Applying this to a society built around a doctrine of unity, the convert finds him/herself struggling to reconcile his/her diverse and seemingly contradictory identities. It has been suggested that conversion out of an ethnic religion, which is likely to be experienced as "inseparable" from the culture in which it is found, as is the case for many people born into Islam in an Arab culture, can lead to an exceptionally great deal of personal and social turmoil (Paper 1999:111-112).

Converts often find it hard, much more than theories built in a Western context often assume, to selectively maintain and present a variety of different identities (McCall and Simmons 1978, Stryker and Serpe 1994, Burke and Stets 2009). Wanting to live a unified life, many are able to root themselves in a national-cultural identification by finding an ethnic identity to match their new religious identities, calling themselves, for example, Arab Christians or Moroccan Christians. Others do work to separate Muslim ethnic identity from Christian religious identity, and try to convince their communities that it is a valid separation. It is a way for them to stay committed to the cohesiveness of the *umma*, maintaining their commitment to their Muslim community while distancing themselves from the faith-based aspects of that affiliation.

Adhesive Identities

An interaction which occurred during many interviews illustrates the tension in negotiating the various identities that come with a faith change in the Arab world. Though the specifics may vary, the following dialogue became quite familiar to me:

Interviewer: "What is your religion? Would you say you're a Christian or a Muslim or something else?"

Participant: "What do you mean? Of course I'm a Christian."[1]

I: "What about your culture, your family, your name?"

P: "No, I haven't changed. I'm still a Muslim completely."

I: "So could you call yourself a Christian Muslim?

P: "No, that would be blasphemous!"

---

[1] The "Insider Movement" had not yet grown sufficiently in the Middle East such that its ideas about converts remaining fully Muslim, had reached many MBBs in the Middle East. I met a few converts who had heard of that ideology and were relatively critical of it. In the few places where I did hear of groups of converts engaging in the "Insider Movement", I was not allowed access in time to include the findings in this study, though as will be presented below, I did meet converts who continued to refer to themselves as "Muslim". The appropriateness of the "Insider Movement" to a Middle Eastern context remains, as far as I have seen, undocumented, whereas the approach described in this section seems to describe well an extensive underground networks of believers. Because these networks are kept secret, their numbers are not known, but as I did my research it became clear that the more I investigated, the more I would find, suggesting that their numbers may be quite large indeed.

Most participants were sure they wanted to be Christian, but recognised a continuity with their Muslim past that they could not, nor did they necessarily want to, break. Selective presentation, or Don't Ask Don't Tell, helps them to live with possibly contradictory identities, but a number of participants told me that they see this as a temporary situation. They plan to move somewhere where they can live as Christian, or they hope that their community will soon come to accept their change. Many just wonder how much longer they will be able to live like this.

This is where symbolic interactionism fails in explaining the dynamics of religious conversion in the Middle East. Symbolic interactionism provides a framework for selective presentation of various roles, but rarely assumes that different roles might exclude each other, or be in direct conflict with each other. Instead, it assumes that the roles that are socially reinforced will be the ones that are emphasised, while the roles that are negatively rewarded socially may fade in importance. By that model, we would expect participants in this study to soon forget about being Christian and return to a fully Muslim life, as that is what is reinforced in their cultural context. While many people do indeed return to Islam, many also do not, instead pursuing a deviant faith even without much social reinforcement. Many people's stories do tell of some reinforcement for their Christian role, but rarely of more reinforcement than negative injunctions.

Fenggang Yang suggested a framework for understanding convert identities which seems to apply well to the identity change of many Muslim-background followers of Christianity. In many ways immigrants face challenges similar to those of religious converts as they begin to question identities that were previously holistic and assumed (Roy 2004:122). Yang did an extensive qualitative study on Chinese immigrant converts to Christianity in the United States, and based on his data and literature on immigrant groups, he suggests that the members of the church he studied developed "adhesive identities". He says that immigration studies have often focused on assimilation, but assimilation assumes that immigrants abandon their ethnicity to some extent, or else are unable to adjust to their new context because they preserve their ethnicity. Instead, he suggests, the immigrants who are most successful in adapting to their new context are those who adopt two simultaneous identities, both of which are of primary importance to the convert.

Chinese converts to Christianity referred to their Christian faith as providing an identity that transcends their other identities if and when they came into conflict with each other (Yang 1999:179). In his research, most people were integrating their Chinese and American identities: their Christian identity became an adhesive which helped them to bind the other two together (Yang 1999:183). There are elements of their Chinese heritage, notably Buddhist practices, that they part with in order to adopt their new identities, but there are many other elements, including various Confucian teachings, that they maintain. They find they do not need to part entirely with their Chinese identity in order to be American, and many find that becoming a Christian and joining a Chinese church helps them make that adjustment. Similarly, in her study of converts to Islam in Scotland, Nicole Bourque reports that among her participants there were varied combinations of religious and cultural Muslim identity, and also ethnic Scottish identity. Similar to Yang, though, she found that Islam, as a religious identity, often transcended their other identities (Bourque 2006:245-246).

Such adaptations are often met with suspicion by people who come from a Christian background, who see non-orthodox expressions of Christianity as religious syncretism. Philip Jenkins tells a story of a Korean woman who adopted Christianity as a faith but claimed that she was part-Buddhist, part-Confucian, and part-Christian. She suggested that everyone adheres multiple identities in such a way, but that they do not admit it (Jenkins 2002:120). As a new faith is adopted into a new context, it is in fact much more common to maintain old practices and incorporate them into the new identity. In Western Christian traditions, for example, pre-Christian European practices have been incorporated into major religious holidays.

Yang identifies three different options that are pursued as people develop their immigrant convert identities. Fragmentary integration describes when someone adopts some values or lifestyles from others but continues to maintain one dominant identity. Fusive integration blends several cultures and melts out distinct characteristics. He says that someone with fusive integration never fits in, seeming too Chinese to Americans and too American to Chinese. Finally, adhesive integration is when people add multiple identities without necessarily losing one, allowing for positive interaction with people in a variety of different social settings (Yang 1999:183-185).

Because Yang's research was in an immigrant community, his categories of identity are slightly different from the categories that are relevant here. He discusses integration of the culture left behind, the culture into which the immigrant is moving, and the religious culture. The participants in this study are integrating their Muslim ethnicity, their religious identity as Christians, and their unique role as converts or religious deviants. We might consider that the unique convert identity that is forming in the Arab world, that which is labelled MBB, or alternately BMB, and *mutanasrin* in Arabic, becomes the adhesive that holds their Muslim ethnic identity and their Christian religious identity together. However, different participants put different degrees of emphasis on these different identities, resulting in different types and levels of integration of their identities.

Yang gave value-based names to the three types of integration, indicating that adhesive integration is the best way to develop an immigrant identity. In my research, it seems that the same might apply to most of the participants in this study, but it also seemed very important for each person to come to his/her own conclusion about how to live as a religious changer, and so I do not want to dismiss people who demonstrated fragmentary or fusive integration, especially when they carefully thought through their own identity change. Some people are relatively new converts and will likely continue to change their identities, but others have made a careful decision to define their identity the way they do. In addition, these cannot be seen as rigid categories, as there were participants that in some ways, or at some times, illustrated one type of identity integration, and at other times a different type.

Fragmentary integration, in which one adopts new characteristics but does not part with a dominant identity, is seen most frequently in the narratives of people who consider their primary identity ethnically, as Muslims. These individuals see themselves as Muslim but as having adopted Christian beliefs or "following Jesus". This was the smallest group among the participants in this project, but is the way conversion is defined within the "Insider Movement". A couple of women see themselves as fully Muslim because they continue committed to the cultural and political values of the community in which they grew up. Therefore, they feel that, were they to claim to adopt "Christianity", they would be abandoning who they are. In a different scenario, one man explained to me that he is still Muslim, but if it were legal for him to become a Christian he would; since it is not, he will remain Muslim. He does not see a way of adopting a new identity so he is continuing with the identity he has.

One woman explained that it was a process for her to be willing to embrace her Muslim identity:

> I am still a Muslim but I follow Christ. I don't want to change my identity, neighbourhood, name, etc. (which is what would happen if I were to become a Christian). For the first year or two I said I was a Christian. It was safer when meeting someone I didn't know before: if I said I was a Christian that was fine, but if I told them I was a Muslim who follows Christ then that would make me an apostate, so I preferred people to think I was a Christian. And I liked Christians... But now I love Islam. I am a Muslim Sunni but I love the Christ and follow him.

In her understanding of identity, in order to continue in her Muslim ethnic identity, she must not associate with Christianity: one nullifies the other. Choosing to retain her Muslim identity places her at higher risk, but she feels it is the right thing to do. She said later in the interview that by not adopting any institutional religion, instead seeing her faith as unrelated to her Muslim-ness, she feels greater freedom in her life to develop religiously and to associate with whomever she likes.

Fusive integration is found in people who place their religious identity ahead of their ethnic identity, seeing themselves as primarily Christians. This seems to be the default for new converts. Like the woman described above, when people change faith they usually see that as a change of everything in their lives. People with fusive integration place a high priority on continuing to develop in their new identity and see their Muslim legal identification as little more than a piece of paper, without regard for their families' or their past history. Some participants told me that they are Christian on the inside even though they still have to be Muslim on the outside. Some of those people have adhesively embraced both their internal and their external identity, while most accept their external identity only as something imposed on them. For some, society's imposition of a Muslim identity pushes them to want to associate even more closely with Christianity. One young man, for example, told me that the more he senses his society insisting that he should be Muslim, the more he insists on being Christian.

Some members of traditional churches who demonstrate fusive identity believe that it is not possible to continue to be Muslim in any way. This was the position of almost all Christians, from or working in the Middle East, only a few decades ago. To them, following Christianity means becoming fully Christian but often find they are unable to do so. One man explained that, although he is not opposed to his relatives continuing to be Muslims, he has changed everything about his life: he is married to a Christian woman, lives in a Christian neighbourhood, wears a large cross around his neck, works at a Christian organisation, and has been repudiated by his non-religious Muslim parents. He said:

> No, I don't at all think of myself as still a Muslim. Muslim people probably think about it, but it never enters my mind. But if I die for Christ, I wouldn't be the first martyr. But I was a Muslim by 'name' only... I found myself in the church!... I don't see myself as Muslim; I'm a follower of Christ. But the reason I'm not a Muslim is because I converted – I pray according to the Christian faith, I don't fast like a Muslim or go to the haj (pilgrimage).

His total change has placed him as an outsider among both Muslims and Christians. Even though he lives the life of a Christian, he still has some qualities, such as his manner of speaking and an estranged family, that set him apart from his Christian in-laws, friends and co-workers; at the same time, he has deliberately become fully an outsider in Muslim communities.

Some members of Protestant churches or people who only participate in small communities of coreligionists have taken a similar approach to identity integration, but overall, those who affiliate with non-traditional Christian groups are less likely to see Christian identity as encompassing all of their lives than converts like this man, who joined a Catholic community. This suggests that Catholic and Orthodox Christianity, which are highly ritualised and have a strong historical presence in the Middle East, are more similar to Middle Eastern Islam in their emphasis on unity and community. Indeed, one of the participants pointed out to me that her community's negative reaction to her commitment to a Christian faith and church is no different from the reaction to someone who leaves a Catholic or Orthodox church in her country to join a Protestant church.

Adhesive integration is much easier to achieve among Muslim-background followers of a Christian faith in contexts where there is not a pre-existing

Christian community, and in places where national identity is not tightly wrapped up in Islamic religious tradition. In North African countries, converts previously saw, for example, their Moroccan or Tunisian identities as including the Muslim religion but not so strongly that leaving Islam to follow Christianity meant that they had to negate their national identity. It feels somewhat fitting to them to become "North African Christian". This is not as easy to do in the Middle East or the Arab gulf nations, though some have tried and seem to succeed in adhering their identities, even in those countries where it is most difficult.[2]

I met a number of participants, from a number of different Arab countries, who demonstrated adhesive identities. One man explained how he continues as a Muslim but has affiliated with Christians in the following way:

> I didn't change anything, I didn't change religions. I just got a new and clearer picture of God... If people say I'm a Muslim, then I'm a Muslim, sure. To me, I am a son of God. Does that have to be a Christian? If so, then I am... I don't think that we have to become Christian, not at all. But it is very important for us to be connected with the Christians. We are mutanasrin, although that's not the best word to use, but if you want to use that word, fine. We are believers from a different background. But we have to be connected with the group of Christians, to learn from them... to be connected with other believers. So it is very important for us to be participating with the Christian group, but that is not the same thing as joining the society of Christians in [my country].

In his account he first emphasised that he did not cease to be a Muslim when he changed faith. He separates his faith from his religion, or perhaps more explicitly, his religion from his ethnicity, which is his ascribed identity. He also expressed that he is willing for others to define his identity as they see fit: some perceive him as a Muslim and others as a Christian. In examples he gave in other parts of his narrative, it is clear that usually it is Muslim acquaintances who see him as Muslim and fellow church-goers who consider him a Christian, so he is able to fit in to some extent in both communities. While he insisted that

---

[2] In the Middle East countries, including Lebanon and Egypt, there is a strong albeit small historical Christian community which functions as a distinct ethnicity. Adhering a Christian identity to a Muslim identity is complicated by the historically difficult relations between Christian and Muslim ethnic groups. The mere word "Christian" feels antagonistic to Muslim-ness, and labels such as "Arab Christian" or "Egyptian Christian" already belong to historical Christians. In most of the Arab gulf region, there are no national non-Muslim religious groups, but it is also where Islam was founded and thus Islam seems to be a particularly essential element of what it means to be from the Arab gulf. Although I did no field research in the Arab gulf region, people I know who have met MBBs from there inform me that they face enormous challenges in adhering a Christian identity onto their Muslim identity, especially because of extremely stringent legal and societal restraints. Many of them may find no alternative to fragmentary integration.

conversion does not mean becoming a Christian in an ethnic sense, he did collectively identify himself with Christians, as he claimed that they are his co-religionists, people he can learn from and with whom he worships. Use of an adhesive label, *mutanasrin*, helped him to further define his identifications.

Many people find it much easier to adhere their identities if they consider their "Christian" identity not as Christian per se, since that is so commonly associated with an ethnicity in their communities. In this sense, many people whose self-identification suggested they were adopting fragmentary integration may actually be adhering their identities but renaming their Christian identity. The woman quoted above who claimed above to be a Muslim and to not have become a Christian did at a different point in her narrative emphasise that she has become a "follower of Christ", explaining:

> The distinction between Christ and Christian is important. Many Muslims may say they wish they were Christian because they like Christian names better, or because Christian neighbourhoods are prettier. But those who are really interested in the faith are also not going to understand the distinction until the Spirit makes it clear to them. Only with God's help can we understand the difference between the faith and the religion. It's an important distinction between saying that I follow Christ, and that I love Christianity.

She has chosen to root her faith identity in the phrase "follow Christ" because she finds that makes a clear distinction between her faith and her affiliation with Christianity as an ethnicity.

What term is used does not matter so much as that a label is used to help adhere otherwise-competing identities. For example, in addition to *mutanasrin* or MBB, or even "follower of Christ", other participants found a collective identity as a member of a "church", carefully avoiding affiliating themselves with the loaded identification of "Christian". However, while that distinction has helped one woman justify her change and reconcile her seemingly contradictory identities to herself, her father saw her decision to join a church as conversion and did not recognise the same distinction. There are no clear rules or guidelines that can be drawn here, rather it is the principle of adhering identities, embracing all of what one is rather than attempting to deny one part in favour of a new part.

It is unlikely that one label will resonate with all converts, and the terms "Christ" and "church" are usually just as controversial and explosive in Muslim communities as "Christian". Some participants said they might as well call themselves "Christian" because calling themselves "followers of Christ" or members of a "church" would result in the same strong reaction. It also bears mentioning that adhesive identities are not a formula for peace. The decision of a Muslim to follow anything associated with Christianity, Christ or the Gospel is controversial and problematic, and no matter how s/he phrases it, there is likely to be a strong adverse reaction to his/her decision when and if it is clearly announced.

Nonetheless, some converts find that their own revulsion at the idea of becoming Christian, who they were always taught were dirty and even murderous, is overcome if they can separate their faith conversion from an affiliation with "Christianity". Furthermore, as discussed in the previous chapter, a great deal of personal change can happen without labelling it. Different families will react differently to such change, but as long as the change is peaceful and honourable, avoiding a label may minimise the controversy, or at least focus it on the issues of the heart rather than names.

In closing, this discussion of adhesive identity might imply that the process of combining different identities is somewhat formulaic, simply a decision a convert needs to make, but such a conclusion does not follow from the evidence. Identity redefinition for religious converts is a complex and long process. Participants told many tales of finding themselves in complicated situations where they did not know how to interact with others, of a high degree of social stress, and of facing personal danger when others did not accept their presentation of their different identities. The difficulty of adhering identities is particularly acute when converts have children and attempt to raise them with the same adhesive identities.

While the theory of adhesive identities helps to conceptualise the process and experience of adapting to a new sense of self within a new faith, the road to adaptation is full of complications and challenges. Many MBBs state that the most difficult challenge they face is that of redefining their identity. Due to all the issues discussed thus far, developing a convert identity is important but difficult. It is made even more difficult by the hope, even expectation, that they will develop a perfect and unified new identity. They expect that their new identity will feel more comfortable to them than their Muslim identity did before they started questioning the religion with which they were raised. Their joy in their new identity could be confirmation that they made the right decision, and so it is difficult to accept that adopting a new identity is so difficult.

In fact, serious emotional and psychological concerns emerge. Anomie, the yearning for something better but a perpetual inability to achieve it, is possibly the most common and troubling expression of these difficulties. A deep sense of disappointment with much about one's new life is another expression. Finally, as people adopt new values and a new sense of self, there is a process of mourning some of the best things about their pre-conversion culture.

Influences on Identity Development

An important factor in developing a convert identity is contact with co-religionists and other converts. Growing into a new religious identity involves interacting with other co-religionists and with others who have a different perspective of their chosen religion (Bourque 2006:237-239). Through such interaction, the convert starts to use the group's rhetoric and language of transformation, which helps development of a new worldview and identity according to what is expected by the new community (Rambo and Farhadian 1999:30). While, as previously discussed, participants in this study joined a variety of different types of religious groups and developed a diversity of relationships with other converts and with Christians, it was clear that their first Christian community was an important factor influencing how they re-defined their identity.

The process of those who converted in traditional churches, especially Catholic or Orthodox, was generally marked by institutional sanction and formal rituals (see Taylor 1999:48). Those who converted by this process usually stayed affiliated with traditional churches and came to have a very fusive integration of their identity as they strove to become fully Christian. Others, however, met other converts early on and followed their lead in adhering their Christian identity onto their Muslim background. There were also participants who spent years without any contact with Christians, and continued to consider themselves fully Muslim although they had an altered faith. Finally, there are converts whom I have heard about but never met because they are determined to develop their identities entirely within Muslim society and without any contact with foreigners or other people who are ethnically Christian. From reports I have heard, these believers usually chose to do so at the advice of a fellow convert or a missionary. It must be noted that different converts I met, although they varied in identity integration and in the advice they had received with regards to how to live out their new faith, did seem to ascribe to a common shared doctrine.

In formulating their new identity, participants were likely to follow the advice of the convert, Christian-born Arab or missionary who became their first mentor. Rarely were they exposed to other ways of thinking about or conceiving an MBB identity. Even though there are a number of different labels which can be assigned to converts and various approaches to identity integration, new believers are rarely aware that they have options from which to choose how to define their new identity. Until stigmatised people can confidently adopt a label, it is difficult for them to grow into their altered identity (Hill 2009:352).

On the other hand, when converts have only one picture of the trajectory their new faith might take, they have a relatively clear sense of structure in a life that very possibly may otherwise be very tumultuous. While this can be helpful for avoiding anomie, it also leaves more space for disappointment when life within this new structure is not perfect.

Different approaches to convert identity are extensively discussed in the missiological literature on Muslim conversions, and most Christians who work with Muslims or with converts are familiar with the idea of different categories of converts.[3] However, most converts I met had never been exposed to any

[3] See Travis 1999 (both) for an explanation of the "C1 to C6 Spectrum", another

variation in approaches to becoming a "Christian" from a "Muslim" background. Many of them had assumed they had no option but to abandon their Muslim background and fully assume a Christian identity, and they were somewhat frustrated that they had not succeeded in doing so. Often, they expressed surprise and hopefulness when they learned of other models for convert identity.

Instead of being exposed to different ideas about identity, most MBBs follow someone's instructions as to how to redefine themselves, regardless of whether they feel comfortable in that identity or not. But many converts made a decision to change faith after making a major examination of the claims of each faith and carefully deciding what doctrine to follow, especially men but also women. Some participants told me that they highly value the importance of thinking and analysing things in life and not just taking them for granted. However, after they have made, and are expected by other Christians to have made, a careful choice, they often find themselves in a situation where other believers give them no choice in developing the various aspects of their new identity: how they live and with whom, how they perceive themselves and how they interact with others in society. This may be related to the belief of most Christians that their own iteration of the Christian life is right. Thus, while converts went through a careful process of analysis and selection of their faith, they are frequently seen by other Christians to have come to the correct decision, and so are expected to naturally follow the "correct" way of living out that decision. Christians, then, may "feed" them what they see as being the only truth in terms of how to live everyday life according to a Christian faith.

Adaptation Processes

As people face their new lives with enthusiasm, they often feel a great deal of hunger to learn as much as they can about their new faith, and to spend as much time as possible with people who share their new faith. This can lead to a "bridge-burning" of relationships with people from the convert's past, in order to have more time to devote to the new identity (Carrothers 2004:16). In a sense, as a person's commitment to his/her new religion increases, so does his/her rejection of others from his/her past. Many participants reported a great hunger to read as much of the Bible as they could, to attend as many church meetings as they could and, when that was not possible, to tune in to religious broadcasting on the radio or on the television. I met people who went to church meetings four or five days a week, in three or more different churches.

One man told me that he left his previous friendships behind when he chose to live as a Christian, which at first bothered him, but eventually he decided that the friendships which replaced them were more intimate, and that he had a

framework commonly used in Christian missionary circles to describe these different potential approaches.

more active social life in his Christian community than he did as a Muslim. Most participants seemed to develop a balance after the excitement of their new faith faded. Many people, even if they break off relations with their families when they declare their new faith, are able to restore those relationships years later, and often they make new Muslim friends even if they do not continue friendships with Muslims they knew before their conversion. A few, however, do maintain such a high involvement with Christian activities that they never return to having regular contact with members of their previous Muslim community. Their choice of relationships continues to play an important role in their definition of their lives as converts.

In studies of conversion to Islam, researchers have found that actions and rituals are also useful in embodying a new identity. Nicole Bourque writes about woman converts, "Every time that a woman would pray, say a *du'a* before entering the bathroom, or provide a good meal for her family, she reaffirmed her decision to live as a Muslim woman. That is, a Muslim identity is embodied through daily bodily practices. Those actions are also important in letting other people see that you are a Muslim" (Bourque 2006:242). In many ways, this is actually much the opposite of the experience of most converts to Christianity. While some quickly begin to attend highly ritualised churches, such as people who lived in monasteries for a time or who quickly learned an Orthodox catechism, many more found that growing into a Christian identity meant unlearning actions and rituals, often without replacing them.

Since one of the appeals of Christianity to many converts was the freedom it gave, they often found that part of their identity reformulation was the process of giving up Muslim rituals. One man told me that it took a while for him to stop reading the Qur'an, but he felt like it was the right thing to do: "Even after I became a believer, there was some kind of respect to it... I used to listen to it, the tone: I really liked to listen to it. I really love the Arabic language. After a time, I felt it's not suitable to do that because the word of the Bible was enough for me." As he grew into his new identity, he considered it important that he part with Muslim rituals. Meanwhile, he had already started reading the Bible, but that did not translate to a full adoption of a set of rituals: his new faith took on a more personal and less ritualised role in his life.

Another man told of how he tried to remove all Muslim terminology from his vocabulary because it was important that he not continue in Muslim religious traditions. He also stopped fasting, but struggled with the realisation that he felt less religious because he did not fast. He said, "I don't want to look like I'm taking the easy way out, which it often seems to [my family], but I do appreciate the freedom I have to not fast from sun up to night during Ramadan."

Converts out of Islam also often go through a period of mourning the loss of their culture. The *tawhid* of life in a tight-knit Muslim community is replaced by a season of life in which they can, and arguably should, re-assess and redefine everything about how they structure their lives. For example, fasting during Ramadan is much more than a religious obligation: it is a culturally-rich season full of rituals and times set aside for family. It is replaced by a doctrine that upholds fasting but gives little guidance as to how to fast. Christian religious holidays are much less ritualised in the Middle East: while a number of traditions and celebrations surround Eid al-Adha and Eid al-Fitr, Christmas and Easter are celebrated through simple activities sponsored by small churches or nuclear families.

Beyond the potentially anomic freedom, there are few other cultural values likely to be obtained through conversion that can replace those that were transmitted in a strongly cohesive family and religious community, unless the convert chooses, and is accepted in, a highly ritualised church. Several participants, for example, mourned the loss of hospitality: they came from families that demonstrate deep and generous hospitality, but they do not see that in their new communities. They do not want to lose this part of their culture, but it is difficult to redefine one's identity while holding on to many strong cultural values of one's past.

So, in conversion from Islam to Christianity, instead of embodying the new identity, rituals often symbolise the identity being left behind. Some converts continue with Muslim rituals, but give them a Christian meaning. One group fasted during Ramadan, but fewer hours per day, and met regularly during that time to pray as a community of converts. Others adopt new rituals, maybe those of the church they attend, maybe by individually designating regular times for reading the Bible. There are also those who simply enjoy the freedom they feel. Many, though, find that this loss of structure leads to a degree of anomie.

Conclusion

Second-Generation Converts

I would like to close this discussion with some words about an issue that emerged over and over again in the course of this research as the single most challenging issue facing Muslim-background Arabs who choose to follow a Christian faith: their children.

While confidently facing myriad personal challenges, many expressed a sense of inner torture when talking about raising their children. Since apostasy is not permitted, children of converts are generally expected to be Muslim, not Christian, and therefore the child of a convert to Christianity is actually a Muslim being raised as a Christian. This is how extended families usually perceive their young relatives, and it is also, in most countries, their legal identification.

So, at the very least, the child of a convert may be a Christian who knows that s/he is different, but usually they are assumed to be Muslim. Most of the challenges that converts face, their children also face. In addition, parents are concerned because their children are facing those challenges without the personal conviction that Christian faith is better than Muslim faith or that a different identity is worth fighting for. One couple, who was expecting their first child when I met them, said that they were afraid for their child's future, and they told me that they had for a while actually prayed that they might prove unable to bear children.

Religious studies have constantly demonstrated that the largest growth in a given religious group is usually biological. If MBBs were to refrain from having children, or raise their children as Muslim, then their small community of converts, the so-called minority-within-a-minority has little chance of growing in size or resilience. Biological growth is what may move this community beyond status as a small "sect", to achieving recognition in their social milieu. The participants in this study did not want to use their children for the cause of religious legitimacy, nor did they want their children to be pulled back into Islam, the religion that they had consciously rejected.

Many participants in this study did not yet have children, and those who did mostly had children younger than school-age. One man who had a one-year old daughter said that he did not have any model to follow in making decisions as to how to raise his daughter: "We try different things, because there is no rule that has been developed about how to raise converts' children. We will have to have different experiences, and look for the Lord to help us." In a sense, he saw his own experiences as a test case, and his daughter's experiences as something that would become an example to others – either of what to do or of what not to do. The vast majority of the converts I have met who have adolescent children or older, left their home countries to live in Christian-majority nations.

One man described well the concerns of many MBBs as he spoke about his own son, who was about three years old: "[Converts] need to be a light to their children, they need to go to church and take their children to church as much as possible... There are all kinds of problems at school – even at the nursery, children are taught Islam. This doesn't work. They can't be taught Christianity at home and Islam at the school... They will get too confused." Because he was concerned that his child would grow up confused, he was reticent to allow his son to visit the grandparents because they teach him Muslim rituals and beliefs. He was also very concerned about where he would send his son to school: he did not want his child to attend a public or a Muslim school, because in those schools he would attend Islam classes. It would be difficult to get his son into a Christian school, because Christian schools rarely accept Muslim students and the tuition fees are higher. His best hope was to persuade a sympathetic school director to allow his son not to attend any religion course, since a Muslim student in his country would not be allowed in Christianity lessons. As this explanation might demonstrate, this man was spending a great deal of mental energy thinking about how to negotiate his son's identity as the son of a convert, indeed a good bit more time than he spent thinking about his own convert identity.

Other participants expressed a strong preference for a school taught with an international, religion-free curriculum, but the one family I met who was able to afford an international school faced serious mental health issues with their two daughters. One learned to manage her different identities so cleverly that she was regularly getting away with other types of cheating, while the other daughter was demonstrating serious emotional disturbance. Her mother took her to a psychologist, and was given a frightening prognosis: "The doctor advised me to leave the country," she explained. "He said that she has schizophrenia, and is developing multiple personalities... He also said that her sister is actually more sick, even though it shows for [the first sister] more now, and we should leave the country so they can get better."

This family's MBB friends were concerned for them, but also for what this might mean for their own, younger and yet-unborn, children: this family was relatively united and cohesive, with both parents sharing a Christian faith, and able to pay for an expensive non-religious education. Even so, they were facing grave problems. If this family's children were in crisis, what was the prognosis for children in less privileged homes?

The challenges and dynamics of child-rearing vary from country to country. The psychologist who saw the girl described above recommended leaving the country because many of the factors contributing to their disturbance would be left behind. Converts who live outside of the Arab world may face conflicts with their children, but usually not conflicts specifically related to being converts, as opposed to the types of challenges facing most immigrants. The two main issues complicating child-rearing for converts in the Arab world are family pressure and government religious identification. Both are no longer concerns if a convert moves to Europe or America.

As parents decide how to raise their children, their approach often reflects closely their own approach to identity integration. For example, people with more fragmentary identity integration, who still see themselves as Muslim, often raise their children as Muslim, only adding occasional visits to church or Bible storytime at night to the upbringing they would be giving them if in a fully Muslim home. However, everyone who was doing so also expressed that they would prefer to raise their children as Christians if it were socially and legally possible. Others seek to raise their children adhesively, with both an awareness of their Muslim heritage but also a knowledge of Christian values or doctrine. One community in North Africa reported that they think this is an ideal approach, because they teach their children to see Islam from a relatively intellectual standpoint, as a part of their country's culture and history. They also regularly take them to a Christian group, read Bible stories to them, and teach them that their family has a faith different from that of most of their friends.

In the Middle East, where Christianity has both a religious and an ethnic meaning, many converts have found teaching children to have adhesive identities to be too difficult and too confusing for the children. Some intend to try to follow the North Africans' example, while most prefer an approach more akin to fusive integration, raising their children as Christian, somewhat sheltered from the struggles they themselves faced in working through their convert identities. One participant, for example, told me that he had not previously planned on trying to find a way to change his legal religious registration, but when he had his first child, he started to investigate the options, because he believes a Christian identity is important for the second generation, who do not understand the nuances of adhesive identities. Such an endeavour was unlikely to succeed, but he was committed to trying because he expected that his children would grow up with a better faith and an easier life if they could simply be Christian.

Others do everything they can to shelter their children from Islam. One couple told me that they do not let their son visit his Muslim cousins or have Muslim friends: they want him to be raised as a Christian child. Another woman told me that she often found herself confronting her family about certain issues, in order to shelter her daughters from their Muslim relatives and their expectations or pressures. Grandparents, aunts and uncles often take great pleasure in teaching the children of their families, and Muslim grandparents, aunts and uncles often teach the children Muslim practices, Qur'anic recitations and other aspects of the religion without concern for how it relates to the

Christian teachings they are receiving from their parents. This is why many families, if they are able, leave the country when their children reach school age, even some who were previously determined to remain committed to their country, extended family, and ethnic Muslim identity. They are willing to take the risk and face the challenges, but they are not willing to put their children through the same.

In countries where it is easier to develop adhesive identities, such as in North Africa (Morocco, Algeria, Tunisia, for example), families may face fewer challenges. One young woman from North Africa who was raised in a convert home told me about years of turmoil and rebellion, but she eventually became a productive member of society, looking back with gratitude to her parents for raising her as a convert child. Similarly, in Lebanon, the only Arab country where it is even possible to legally change religion, families are not as concerned as they are in countries like Egypt, where it has not thus far been possible. Religious schooling is not a problem in Lebanon, and a change in legal registration is a signal to the extended family that there has been a change. Even so, many of the same issues remain, if with a bit less intensity.

In various Arab contexts, Christians and MBBs alike have expressed concern that conversion might not be carried through generations: children may revert to Islam as the social default in their society, carrying with them the emotional scars of dealing with identity negotiation at a young age.

In fact, many converts report that, while they strongly desire for their children to follow in their spiritual footsteps, it is even more important to them that they raise their children with an ability to make decisions for themselves and to be tolerant. Some participants who had not actually changed faith, but who had attended church and taken their children to Sunday school, said that their exploration of Christianity had had a definite effect on their children. They saw their children as more tolerant and open to new ideas than they otherwise would have been, even if they remained Muslim. One woman MBB told me that her greatest dream for her daughter is for her to make good decisions. She wants her daughter to choose Christianity, but the mother feels that it is more important for her to grow up with a sense of freedom and independence: "As I decided in my life, she has the freedom to choose her own path... it will be her decision. Of course, I'll fight not to let her go another way; I'll fight by logic, using my own weapons. I will raise her as a Christian, but accept her decision." She believes that good parenting must involve religious education in keeping with the parents' convictions, but that that should not mean that their children grow up feeling like they have no choice but to follow their parents' path.

Her opinion was echoed by several other participants, including some who said that growing up with any religious foundation is possibly more important than which religion is being taught. Other participants said that they intended to raise their children without any specific religious education, at least not during early childhood. They preferred to give their children a secular education, which would include Christian values but not push Christianity, so that their children could make their own choice later in life. One man explained that if he is living in a setting where his children are required by law to receive Muslim education, he will try to counteract that at home by teaching what he sees as wrong with Islam, but he will emphasise their ability to choose what they believe. He believes that the best way to teach his children about his own Christian faith is to live according to Christian values and be an example, rather than teaching them religious doctrine.

Whose Risk? Whose Dream?

As I think back across the various things I've learned through this study, I reflect on how complicated it is to adjust to a new life. While adjusting to a new identity is akin to adjusting to a new set of skin, even more difficult is realising that this new skin may not be as comfortable or as pleasant as the old one. Converts from Islam to a Christian faith who stay the course of faith over years and decades, are usually very convinced and impassioned about what they believe.

They still hold on to their dreams, believing that heaven is not only for the afterlife but it is for the real world as well. All the converts whom I met had experienced feeling Jesus' presence with them, or comforting dreams at times when they were particularly emotionally vulnerable, or another believer saying just the right thing at the right time. I was inspired by how many of them wanted to make a difference in poverty alleviation, education or community development: the message of Christ that they wanted to bring to their Muslim neighbours was not just a message of doctrine, but it was a message that life can be better here on this earth, today. After all, even with the challenges they faced, they themselves experienced a bit of heaven in their everyday lives through their experience of their new faith. The strength behind such love lay somewhere in the intersection of their strong value-based upbringing in Islam, and their new faith in Jesus.

I also saw the fall-out of stress and emotional suffering. Living with mixed identities is not easy, and I met many people who dreamed of doing great things: serving the Poor, preaching the Gospel, bringing together the converts of their country into a unified new *umma*. But as often as not they fell short of their goals for themselves. Legal harassment, family obligations, and struggling against the social order of their communities held them back. But I also saw exhaustion and stress, a weariness that came from investing so much energy in themselves: their own identity, their own relationships, their own well-being.

No, this is not an easy path to walk. Converts desire Christianity but they do not desire to abandon Muslim community. They have a rebellious spirit, but they are also fiercely loyal to the very people from whom they wish to rebel. They want to live in *umma* but they thrive in individualism. They wish to be embraced into a Christian community and absorb the knowledge of more-experienced believers, but they are also determined to make their own decisions for themselves. They present different pictures of themselves to different groups, often very cleverly. But it is hard to live with dualism.

Determining when people need guidance, and when they need to be given the space to think issues out well on their own, may be one of the most difficult challenges for people, mature converts or born Christians, who work with new converts. People who have seen down the road have a good idea of the challenges that new believers can expect, but they cannot make the choices for their new fellow believers. If we know that remaining in one's Muslim community will make child-rearing painfully difficult, do we still present it to them as a valid and responsible choice? If we know that disappointment and anomie are waiting at the doors of a traditional church, do we point out the benefits of joining Christian community?

There is a great deal of comfort that comes from converts spending time with each other, but if not held in check this can become a source of in-group bias, prejudice against others and cliquishness. At the same time, family is important, and people need the space to relate to their families and home communities in the way that is most appropriate for their cultures and consciences.

When we consider the attention that East-West tension has received in recent decades, and which shows no signs of abating, converts out of Islam are keenly aware of their position in the middle of a geopolitical debate. They are sensitive to being objectified and want to be treated like normal people. At the same time, they may want to be treated as special, unique for the particular challenges that confront them as converts. Ultimately, their identity as believers in Christ is something they share equally with Christians around the world, regardless of the label given. They are not a phenomenon and, without dismissing the the very real and difficult challenges they face, it is important to also recall that difficulties are a part of life and putting people on a platform of admiration for their hard lives, objectifies them as much as does dismissal as the "other".

There is a strong tendency in relations between Western Christians, Arab Christians, and MBBs, to define people as "insiders" and "outsiders" in a variety of different ways. But we are all insiders, and we are all outsiders. Though labels will and should vary, the umbrella of a shared faith should be a bond that brings people together rather than a space in which to further divide. At the same time, each individual, each family, each village and city, each country, represents a unique set of experiences and challenges. We are all outsiders to the experiences of others.

One of the saddest things I learned in my research was that converts were often swept into a Christian community, or a Muslim community devoted to Jesus, and never encouraged to meet converts who were outside of that community, much less Christians from other backgrounds. For some people, life is by choice or by necessity limited to a small geographic and social circle, but for others, such limited interaction easily translates to power plays and attempts to hold control over a group of people. On the other hand, people facing the identity and community challenges outlined in this study can benefit from the wisdom of different voices who have had different experiences and negotiated similar challenges in different ways.

Outsiders often wish to help, but decisions about how to create heaven in this life are the converts' choice. Their decision to adopt a Christian faith was their own, and their decisions as to how to live out the choice that they made are also their own. Many apostates are inherently suspicious: if they deviated out of Islam, surely others are capable of committing deviant acts on behalf of Islam. Then, people whom they thought they could trust disappointed them. Converts too often feel infringed upon by Christians, those whose identity in a Christian faith is secure, on one side, and by Muslims, who are part of the dominant structure of their society, on the other side. When they are inherently suspicious it is difficult to accept help, and on some level they are right, that their problems are their own to resolve. Their risks are their own to take. Others can do little to curtail the risk and should do little to aggravate the risk.

The more I have explored the realities facing this group of people, the more I am reminded that family, community, identity, and faith are issues that all people consider through the course of life. On one hand, this is a particularly under-researched community. The dialogue and writing about conversion out of Islam takes place in the media, in religious circles, but rarely in academia. I believe more research in this tradition is sorely needed. At the same time, though, I hold out hope that increased research may help to de-sensationalise the phenomenon of conversion out of Islam to a Christian faith. Conversion is conversion, and it is always welcome when someone is converting to one's own religion (and sorely disappointing when the convert is apostasising out of one's own religion). In response to the claims of Muslim intellectuals and Christian missionaries alike, I close by suggesting that the results of a decision to leave Islam should be studied in those terms: as something that happens.

Bibliography

Accad, Fouad Elias. 1997. *Building Bridges*. Colorado Springs: NavPress.

Ahmed, Akbar S. 2003. *Islam Under Siege*. Oxford: Polity Press.

Ahmed, Leila. 1992. *Women and Gender in Islam*. London: Yale University Press.

Albrecht, Stan L., Marie Cornwall, and Perry H. Cunningham. 1988. "Religious Leave-Taking: Disengagement and Disaffiliation among Mormons." Pp. 62-80 in *Falling From the Faith: Causes and Consequences of Religious Apostasy*, edited by David G. Bromley. London: Sage Publications.

Alexander, Claire E. 2000. *The Asian Gang: Ethnicity, Identity and Masculinity*. Oxford: Berg.

Allievi, Stefano. 1999. "Pour une sociologie des conversions lorsque des Européens deviennent musulmans." *Social Compass* 46: 283-300.

—. 2002. "Converts and the Making of European Islam." *ISIM Newsletter* 11: 1, 26.

Ameli, Saied Reza. 2002. *Globalization, Americanization, and British Muslim Identity*. London: Icas Press.

Anderson, Mary B. 1999. *Do No Harm: How Aid can Support Peace – or War*. Boulder, CO: Lynne Rienner Publications.

Antoun, Richard. 1972. *Arab Village*. Bloomington: Indiana: University Press.

Appell, G. N. 1978. *Ethical Dilemmas in Anthropological Inquiry: A Case Book*. Waltham, MA: Crossroads Press.

Aravanitakis, James. 2012. "Colonialism and the Emergence of Hope: The Use of Creative Non-Fiction to Reflect on a Society in Transformation." in *Emergent Writing Methodologies in Feminist Studies*, edited by Livholts, Mona. London: Routledge.

Armstrong, Elizabeth. 2002. *Forging Gay Identities*. London: The University of Chicago Press.

Armstrong, Karen. 2002. *Islam: A Short History*. London: Phoenix Press.

—. 2006. *Muhammad: A Prophet for our Time*. New York: Harper Collins.

Asad, Talal. 2003. *Formulations of the Secular: Christianity, Islam, Modernity*. Stanford, CA: Stanford University Press.

Atkinson, Paul, and Sara Delamont. 2006. "Rescuing Narrative from Qualitative Research." *Narrative Inquiry* 16: 164-172.

Ayoub, Mahmoud. 1991. "Islam and Christianity between Tolerance and Acceptance." *Islam and Christian-Muslim Relations* 2: 171-181.

Baker, William G. 2003. *Arabs, Islam, and the Middle East*. Dallas: Brown Books Publishing Group.

Barakat, Halim. 1985. "The Arab Family and the Challenge of Social Transformation." Pp. 27-48 in *Women and the Family in the Middle East*, edited by Elizabeth Fernea. Austin: University of Texas Press.

Barker, Irwin R., and Raymond F. Currie. 1985. "Do Converts Always Make the Most Committed Christians?" *Journal for the Scientific Study of Religion* 24: 305-313.

Baron, Stephen W. 2011. "Street Youths and the Proximate and Contingent Causes of Instrumental Crime: Untangling Anomie Theory." *Justice Quarterly* 28: 413-436.

Barth, Frederik. 1966. *Process and Form in Social Life*. London: Routledge and Kegan Paul.

Baumer, Eric P. and Regan Gustafson. 2007. "Social Organization and Instrumental Crime: Assessing the Empirical Validity of Classic and Contemporary Anomie Theories." *Criminology* 45: 617-663.

Becker, Howard S. 1991 (originally published 1963). *Outsider: Studies in the Sociology of Deviance*. New York: The Free Press.

Bennett, Clinton. 2010. *Muslim Women of Power: Gender, Politics and Culture in Islam*. London: Continuum Publishing Group.

Benson, Peter and Kedron Thomas. 2010. "After Cultural Competency: Research Practice and Moral Experience in the Study of Brand Pirates and Tobacco Farmers." *Qualitative Research* 10: 679-697.

Berben, Raquel Kennedy. 1993. "Interviewing Survivors of Marital Rape: Doing Feminist Research on Sensitive Topics." Pp. 197-211 in *Researching Sensitive Topics*, edited by Claire M. Renzetti and Raymond M. Lee. London: Sage Publications.

Berger, Peter. 1981. "The Pluralistic Situation and the Coming Dialogue between the World Religions." *Buddhist-Christian Studies* 1: 31-41.

Berger, Peter, and Thomas Luckmann. 1966. *The Social Construction of Reality*. Middlesex: Penguin Books.

Beyer, Peter. 1994. *Religion and Globalization*. London: Sage Publications.

—. 2003. "Constitutional Privilege and Constituting Pluralism: Religious Freedom in National, Global, and Legal Context." *Journal for the Scientific Study of Religion* 42: 333-339.

Bhattacharya, Himika. 2008. "New Critical Collaborative Ethnography." in *Handbook of Emergent Methods*, edited by Sharlene Nagy Hess-Biber and Patricia Leavy. London: The Guilford Press.

Bourdieu, Pierre. 1965. Pp. 191-241 in *Honour and Shame*, edited by J.G. Peristiany. London: Weidenfeld and Nicolson.

—. 1977. *Outline of a Theory of Practice*. Cambridge: Cambridge University Press.

Bourdieu, Pierre, and Richard Nice, transl. 2000. *Pascalian Meditations*. Stanford: Stanford University Press.

Bourque, Nicole. 2006. "How Deborah Became Aisha: The Conversion Process and the Creation of Female Muslim Identity." Pp. 233-249 in

Women Embracing Islam, edited by Karin van Nieuwkerk. Austin: University of Texas Press.

Bowser, Benjamin P., and Joan E. Sieber. 1993. "AIDS Prevention Research: Old Problems and New Solutions." Pp. 160-176 in *Researching Sensitive Topics*, edited by Claire M. Renzetti and Raymond M. Lee. London: Sage Publications.

Braithwaite, John. 2010. *Anomie and Violence*. Canberra: ANU E Press.

Brooks, Geraldine. 1994. *Nine Parts of Desire: The Hidden World of Islamic Women*. London: Anchor Books.

Brown, Malcolm. 2010. "Representations of Islamic Fundamentalism and the Ahmed Zaoui Case." *Islam and Christian-Muslim Relations*. 21: 331-341.

Brown, Rick. 2000. "The 'Son of God': Understanding the Messianic Titles of Jesus." *International Journal of Frontier Missions* 17: 41-52.

Bruce, Steve. 1999. *Choice and Religion*. Oxford: Oxford University Press.

Burke, Peter J. 1991. "Identity Processes and Social Stress." *American Sociological Review* 56: 836-849.

Burke, Peter J., and Jan E. Stets. 1999. "Trust and Commitment through Self-Verification." *Social Psychology Quarterly* 62: 347-366.

—. 2009. *Identity Theory*. Oxford: Oxford University Press.

Bybee, Jane A., Eric L. Sullivan, Erich Zielonka, Elizabeth Moes. 2009. "Are Gay Men in Worse Mental Health than Heterosexual Men? The role of Age, Shame and Guilt, and Coming-Out." *Journal of Adult Development* 16: 144-154.

Campbell, J.K. 1965. "Honour and the Devil." Pp. 139-170 in *Honour and Shame*, edited by J.G. Peristiany. London: Weidenfeld and Nicolson.

Carnelley, Katherine B., Erica G. Hepper, Colin Hicks, William Turner. 2011. "Perceived parental reactions to coming out, attachment, and romantic relationship views." *Attachment and Human Development* 13: 217-236.

Carrothers, Robert M. 2004. "Identity Consequences of Religious Conversion: Applying Identity Theory to Religious Changing." Pp. 109 in *Department of Sociology*. Kent, OH: Kent State University.

—. 2010. "Identity Consequences of Religious Changing: Effects of Motivation for Change on Identity Outcomes" *Sociological Focus* 43: 150-162.

Cao, Liqun, Ruohui Zhao, Ling Ren, Jihong "Solomon" Zhao. 2010. "Social Support and Anomie: A Multilevel Analysis of Anomie in Europe and North America." *International Journal of Offender Therapy and Comparative Criminology* 54: 625-639.

Cassell, Joan. 1980. "Ethical Principles for Conducting Fieldwork." *American Anthropologist* 82: 28-41.

Castells, Manuel. 1997. *The Power of Identity*. Oxford: Blackwell Publishers.

Chao, Hsin-Kuang. 2006. "Conversion to Protestantism among Urban Immigrants in Taiwan." *Sociology of Religion* 67: 193-204.

Chapman, Colin. 1995. *Cross and Crescent*. Leicester: Inter-Varsity Press.

Charmaz, Kathy. 2008. "Grounded Theory as an Emergent Method." in *Handbook of Emergent Methods*, edited by Sharlene Nagy Hess-Biber and Patricia Leavy. London: The Guilford Press.

Chase, Susan. 1995. "Taking Narrative Seriously: Consequences for Method and Theory in Interview Studies." Pp. 1-26 in *Interpreting Experience: The Narrative Study of Lives*, edited by Ruthellen Josselson and Amia Lieblich. London: Sage Publications.

Christensen, Jens. 1977. *The Practical Approach to Muslims*. Marseilles: Mrs. M. Christensen and the North Africa Mission.

Clinard, Marshall, ed. 1964. *Anomie and Deviant Behavior*. London: Collier-Macmillan Limited.

Cook-Huffman, Celia. 2008. "The Role of Identity in Conflict." Pp. 19-31 in *Handbook of Conflict Analysis and Resolution*, edited by Dennis J.D. Sandole. London: Taylor and Francis.

Cooper, Anne. 1985. *Ishmael My Brother*. Bromley, Kent: MARC Europe.

Cragg, Kenneth. 1975. *The House of Islam*. Belmont, CD: Wadsworth Publishing Company.

—. 1980. "Conversion and Convertibility." Pp. 193-208 in *Down to Earth: Studies in Christianity and Culture*, edited by J.R.W. Stott and R. Coote. Grand Rapids, MI: William B. Eerdmans Publishing Company.

Curry, Andrew. 2002. "The First Holy War." in *U.S. News and World Report*.

Dahl, Ulrika. 2012. "The Road to Writing: An Ethno(Bio)Graphic Memoir." in *Emergent Writing Methodologies in Feminist Studies*, edited by Livholts, Mona. London: Routledge.

Danish, Ishtiyaq. 1988. "Contextualization: A New Missionary Approach to Muslims." in *al Tawhid*.

D'Augelli, Anthony R. 1998. "Developmental Implications of Victimization of Lesbian, Gay, and Bisexual Youths." Pp. 187-210 in *Stigma and Sexual Orientation*, edited by Gregory M. Herek. London: Sage Publications.

Davie, Grace. 1994. *Religion in Britain since 1945: Believing without Belonging*. Oxford: Blackwell

Davis, Thomas W.D. 2011. *Human Rights in Asia*. Surrey: Edward Elgar Publishing.

deSilva, David A. 1994. "Despising Shame: A Cultural-Anthropological Investigation of the Epistle to the Hebrews." *Journal of Biblical Literature* 113: 439-461.

—. 2000. *Honor, Patronage, Kinship and Purity*. Downers Grove, IL: InterVarsity Press.

DiPlacido, Joanne. 1998. "Minority Stress Among Lesbians, Gay Men, and Bisexuals." Pp. 138-159 in *Stigma and Sexual Orientation*, edited by Gregory M. Herek. London: Sage Publications.

Dodd, Peter C. 1973. "Family Honor and the Forces of Change in Arab Society." *International Journal of Middle East Studies* 4: 40-54.

Downes, David, and Paul Rock. 2003. *Understanding Deviance*. Oxford: Oxford University Press.

Du Bois, Barbara. 1983. "Passionate Scholarship: Notes on Values, Knowing and Method in Feminist Social Science." Pp. 105-116 in *Theories of Women's Studies*, edited by Gloria Bowles and Renate Duelli Klein. London: Routledge and Kegan Paul.

Durkheim, Emile. 1952. *Suicide: a study in sociology*. London: Routledge & Kegan Paul.

—. 1974. "excerpt from "The Elementary Forms of the Religious Life"." Pp. 301-324 in *Classical Approaches to the Study of Religion*, edited by Jacques Waardenburg. Paris: Walter de Gruyter.

—. 2001. *The Elementary Forms of the Religious Life*. Oxford: Oxford University Press.

Dutch, Bernard. 2000. "Should Muslims Become 'Christians'?" *International Journal of Frontier Missions* 17: 15-24.

Ebaugh, Helen Rose Fuchs. 1988. "Leaving Catholic Convents: Toward a Theory of Disengagement." Pp. 110-121 in *Falling From the Faith: Causes and Consequences of Religious Apostasy*, edited by David G. Bromley. London: Sage Publications.

Edwards, Rosalind. 1993. "An Education in Interviewing: Placing the Researcher and the Researched." Pp. 181-196 in *Researching Sensitive Topics*, edited by Claire M. Renzetti and Raymond M. Lee. London: Sage Publications.

Erikson, Eric. 1968. *Identity: Youth and Crisis*. London: Faber and Faber.

Faour, Muhammad. 1991. "The Demography of Lebanon: a Reappraisal." *Middle Eastern Studies* 27:631-641.

Fielding, Nigel G. 1993. "Mediating the Message: Affinity and Hostility in Research on Sensitive Topics." Pp. 146-159 in *Researching Sensitive Topics*, edited by Claire M. Renzetti and Raymond M. Lee. London: Sage Publications.

Fisk, Robert. 1990. *Pity the Nation*. Oxford: Oxford University Press.

Finch, Janet. 1993. "'It's Great to have Someone to Talk to': Ethics and Politics of Interviewing Women." in *Social Research: Philosophy, Politics and Practice*, edited by Martyn Hammersley. London: Sage.

Foucault, Michel. 1986. "Governamentality." *Ideology and Consciousness* 6: 5-21.

Freston, Paul. 2000. "The Road to Damascus: Global Dimensions of Religious Conversion Today." Pp. 77-92 in *Previous Convictions*, edited by Martyn Percy. London: SPCK.

Garces, Nicholas. 2010. "Islam, Till Death Do You Part: Rethinking Apostasy Laws under Islamic Law and International Legal Obligations." *Southwestern Journal of International Law* 16: 229-264.

Gaston, Sarah N., and Amanda Zweerink. 2004. "Ethnography online: 'Natives' practicing and inscribing community." *Qualitative Research* 4: 179-200.

Gaudeul, Jean-Marie. 1999. *Called from Islam to Christ*. London: Monarch Books.

Geertz, Clifford. 1983. *Local Knowledge*. London: Fontana Press.

Giddens, Anthony. 1991. *Modernity and Self-Identity*. Cambridge: Polity Press.

Goddard, Hugh. 1994. "Modern Pakistani and Indian Muslim Perceptions of Christianity." *Islam and Christian-Muslim Relations* 5: 165-188.

—. 2000. *A History of Christian-Muslim Relations*. Edinburgh: Edinburgh University Press.

Goffman, Erving. 1963. *Stigma*. London: Penguin Books.

—. 1983. "The Interaction Order: American Sociological Association, 1982 Presidential Address." *American Sociological Review* 48: 1-17.

Gooren, Henri. 2007. "Reassessing Conventional Approaches to Conversion: Toward a New Synthesis." *Journal for the Scientific Study of Religion*. 46: 337-353.

Greenhalgh, Trisha, and Brian Hurwitz. 1998. *Narrative Based Medicine*. London: BMJ Books.

Greenlee, David H., ed. 2005. *From the Straight Path to the Narrow Way*. Milton Keynes, Bucks: Authentic.

Gubrium, Jaber F. and James A. Holstein. 2008. "Narrative Ethnography." in *Handbook of Emergent Methods*, edited by Sharlene Nagy Hess-Biber and Patricia Leavy. London: The Guilford Press.

Haddad, Yvonne Yazbeck. 2006. "The Quest for Peace in Submission: Reflections on the Journey of American Women Converts to Islam." Pp. 19-47 in *Women Embracing Islam*, edited by Karin van Nieuwkerk. Austin: University of Texas Press.

Halverson, Jeffrey R., H.L. Goodall Jr., Steven R. Corman. 2011. *Master Narratives of Islamist Extremism*. New York: Palgrave MacMillan.

Hammer, Juliana. 2000. "Prayer, Hijab and the Intifada: The Influence of the Islamic Movement on Palestinian Women." *Islam and Christian-Muslim Relations* 11: 299-320.

Hammond, Phillip E. 1988. "Religion and the Persistence of Identity." *Journal for the Scientific Study of Religion* 27: 1-11.

Hammond, Phillip E., and Kee Warner. 1993. "Religion and Ethnicity in Late-Twentieth Century America." *Annals of the American Academy of Political and Social Science* 527, Religion in the Nineties: 55-66.

Harik, Iliya. 1966. "The Maronite Church and Political Change in Lebanon." Pp 31-55 in *Politics in Lebanon*, edited by Leonard Binder. New York: Wiley and Sons.

Heelas, Paul, and Linda Woodhead. 2005. *The Spiritual Revolution: Why Religion is Giving Way to Spirituality*. Oxford: Blackwell Publishing.

Hess-Biber, Sharlene Nagy and Patricia Leavy. 2008. *Handbook of Emergent Methods*. London: The Guilford Press.

Hiebert, Paul G. 1994. *Anthropological Reflections on Missiological Issues*. Grand Rapids, MI: Baker Books.

—. 2005. "Worldview Transformation." Pp. 23-34 in *From the Straight Path to the Narrow Way*, edited by David H. Greenlee. Milton Keynes, Bucks: Authentic.

Hill, Natalie L. 2009. "Affirmative Practice and Alternative Sexual Orientations: Helping Clients Navigate the Coming Out Process." *Clinical Social Work Journal* 37: 346-356.

Hitti, Philip K., transl. 1964. *Memoirs of an Arab-Syrian Gentleman, Memoirs of Usama Ibn-Mundquieth*. Beirut: Khayats Oriental Reprints.

Hitti, Philip K. 2002. *History of the Arabs*. Basingstoke, Hampshire: Palgrave Macmillan.

Hoover, Kenneth. 1997. *The Power of Identity: Politics in a New Key*. Chatham, NJ: Chatham House Publishers.

Hutnik, Nimmi. 1985. "Aspects of Identity in a multi-ethnic society." *New Community* 12: 298-309.

—. 1991. *Ethnic Minority Identity*. Oxford: Clarendon Press.

Iannaccone, Laurence R. 1990. "Religious Capital: A Human Capital Approach." *Journal for the Scientific Study of Religion* 27: 297-314.

—. 1992. "Sacrifice and Stigma: Reducing Free-riding in Cults, Communes, and Other Collectives." *The Journal of Political Economy* 100: 271-291.

—. 1994. "Why Strict Churches are Strong." *The American Journal of Sociology* 99: 1180-1211.

—. 1995. "Risk, Rationality, and Religious Portfolios." *Economic Inquiry* XXXIII: 285-297.

Jacobs, Janet Liebman. 1989. *Divine Disenchantment*. Indianapolis: Indiana University Press.

Jacobsen, Karen, and Loren B. Landau. 2003. "The Dual Imperative in Refugee Research: Some Methodological and Ethical Considerations in Social Science Research on Forced Migration." *Disasters* 27: 185-206.

Jarvie, I.C. 1969. "The Problem of Ethical Integrity in Participant Observation." *Current Anthropology* 10: 505-508.

Jasper, James A. 2007. "Cultural Approaches in the Sociology of Social Movements." in *Handbook of Social Movements Across Disciplines*, edited by Bert Klandermans and Conny Roggeband, eds. 2007. New York: Springer.

Jenkins, Philip. 2002. *The Next Christendom*. Oxford: Oxford University Press.

Jenkins, Richard. 1996. *Social Identity*. London: Routledge.

Jindra, Ines W. 2011. "How Religious Content Matters in Conversion Narratives to Various Religious Groups." *Sociology of Religion* 72:3.

Josselson, Ruthellen. 1990. *Finding Herself*. Oxford: Jossey-Bass Publications.

—. 2004. "The Hermeneutics of Faith and the Hermeneutics of Suspicion." *Narrative Inquiry* 14: 1-28.

Kahn, Richard, and Douglas Kellner. 2003. "Internet Subcultures and Oppositional Politics." Pp. 299-314 in *The Post-Subcultures Reader*, edited by David Muggleton and Rupert Weinzierl. Oxford: Berg.

Karim, Jamillah. 2009. *American Muslim Women: Negotiating Race, Class, and Gender within the Ummah*. London: New York Press.

Kateregga, Badru D., and David W. Shenk. 1997. *A Muslim and a Christian in Dialogue*. Scottdale, PA: Herald Press.

Katz, Cindi. 1994. "Playing the Field: Questions of Fieldwork in Geography." *Professional Geographer* 46: 67-72.

Kelly, Brendan D. 2010. "Globalisation, Psychiatry and Human Rights: New Challenges for the 21st Century." Pp. 3-14 in *Clinical Topics in Cultural Psychiatry*, edited by Rahul Bhattacharya, Sean Cross and Dinesh Bhugra. London: RCPsych Publications.

Khalaf, Samir. 2003. "On Roots and Routes: The Reassertion of Primordial Loyalties." Pp. 107-141 in *Lebanon in Limbo*, edited by Theodor Hanf and Nawaf Salam. Baden-Baden: Nomos Verlagsgesellschaft.

Khaldun, Ibn. 1967. *The Muqaddimah*. Chichester, W. Sussex: Princeton University Press.

Khalidi, Tarif. 1985. *Classical Arab Islam*. Princeton: The Darwin Press.

—. 2001. *The Muslim Jesus*. London: Harvard University Press.

Klandermans, Bert and Conny Roggeband, eds. 2007. *Handbook of Social Movements Across Disciplines*. New York: Springer.

Klein, Renate Duelli. 1983. "How to do what we want to do: thoughts about feminist methodology." Pp. 88-104 in *Theories of Women's Studies*, edited by Gloria Bowles and Renate Duelli Klein. London: Routledge and Kegan Paul.

Kraft, Kathryn. 2010. "Faith is Lived out in Community: Questions of New Community for Arab Muslims who have Embraced a Christian Faith." *St. Francis Magazine* 6:6.

Lamb, Christopher, and M. Darrol Bryant, eds. 1999. *Religious Conversion: Contemporary Practices and Controversies*. London: Cassell.

Lazar, Aryeh, Shlomo Kravetz, and Peri Frederich-Kedem. 2002. "The Multidimensionality of Motivation for Jewish Religious Behavior: Content, Structure, and Relationship to Religious Identity." *Journal for the Scientific Study of Religion* 41: 509-519.

Lazerwitz, Bernard. 1973. "Religious Identification and Its Ethnic Correlates: A Multivariate Model." *Social Forces* 52: 204-220.

Levy, Reuben. 1965. *The Social Structure of Islam*. Cambridge: Cambridge University Press.

Lewis, Bernard. 2003. *The Crisis of Islam: Holy War and Unholy Terror*. London: Phoenix.

Lewis, Bernard and Churchill. 2009. *Islam: The Religion and the People*. New Jersey: Wharton School Publishing.

Lewis, Philip. 2002. *Islamic Britain: Religion, Politics and Identity Among British Muslims*. London: I. B. Taurus & Co. Ltd.

—. 2007. *Young, British and Muslim*. London: Continuum

Librett, Mitch and Dina Perrone. 2010. "Apples and Oranges: Ethnography and the IRB." *Qualitative Research* 10: 729-747.

Livholts, Mona. 2012. *Emergent Writing Methodologies in Feminist Studies*. London: Routledge.

Livingstone, Greg. 1993. *Planting Churches in Muslim Cities*. Grand Rapids, MI: Baker Book House.

Lofland, John, and Rodney Stark. 1965. "Becoming a World-Saver: A Theory of Conversion to a Deviant Perspective." *American Sociological Review* 30: 862-875.

Luckmann, Thomas. 1967. *The Invisible Religion*. London: Collier-Macmillan.

Lyons, M.C., transl. 1971. *Ayyubids, Mamlukes and Crusaders, Tarikh al-Duwal wa'l Muluk of Ibn Al-Furat*. Cambridge: W. Hefferand Sons Ltd.

Makari, Peter E. 2007. *Conflict and Cooperation: Christian-Muslim Relations in Contemporary Egypt*. Syracuse, NY: Syracuse University Press.

Makdisi, Ussama. 2008. *Artillery of Heaven*. London: Cornell University Press.

Makris, G.P. 2007. *Islam in the Middle East: A Living Tradition*. Oxford: Blackwell Publishing.

Malinowski, Bronislaw. 1974. "excerpt from "The Study of 'Primitive Man' and His Religion"." Pp. 545-559 in *Classical Approaches to the Study of Religion*, edited by Jacques Waardenburg. Paris: Walter de Gruyter.

Marshall, David. 1999. *God, Muhammad and the Unbelievers*. Surrey: Curzon Press.

—. 2001. "Christianity in the Qu'ran." in *Islamic Interpretations of Christianity*, edited by Lloyd Ridgeon. Surrey: Curzon Press.

Massey, Joshua. 2000. "God's Amazing Diversity in Drawing Muslims to Christ." *International Journal of Frontier Missions* 17: 5-14.

Matheny, Tim. 1981. *Reaching the Arabs*. Pasadena, CA: William Carey Library.

Mattingly, Cheryl. 2005. "Toward a Vulnerable Ethics of Research Practice." *Health* 9: 453-471.

Mawdudi, Abul Ala. 1994. "The Punishment of the Apostate According to Islamic Law." in *http://answering-islam.org.uk/Hahn/Mawdudi*, edited by Syed Silas Husain and Ernest Hahn: accessed 14/12/2006.

May, John D'Arcy. 2003. *Transcendence and Violence: The encounter of Buddhist, Christian and Primal Traditions*. London: Continuum Publishing Group.

May, William. 1980. "Doing Ethics: The Bearing of Ethical Theories on Fieldwork." *Social Problems* 27: 358-370.

McAuliffe, Jane Dammen. 1999. "Christians in the Qur'an and Tafsir." Pp. 105-121 in *Muslim Perceptions of Other Religions*, edited by Jacques Waardenburg. Oxford: Oxford University Press.

McCall, George, and J. L. Simmons. 1978. *Identities and Interactions*. London: The Free Press.

McIlroy, David. 2005. "Honour and Shame." *Cambridge Papers* 14: 1-4.

Mernissi, Fatima. 1991. *The Veil and the Male Elite*. New York: Addison-Wesley Publishing Company.

—. 1991. *Women and Islam*. Oxford: Blackwell.

—. 2003. *Beyond the Veil*. London: Saqi Books.

Mernissi, Fatema. 2002. *Islam and Democracy*. Cambridge, MA: Perseus Publishing.

Merton, Robert K. 1968. *Social Theory and Social Structure*. London: the Free Press.

Michel, Thomas. 1997. "Social and Religious Factors Affecting Muslim-Christian Relations." *Islam and Christian-Muslim Relations* 8: 53-66.

Mies, Maria. 1983. "Towards a methodology for feminist research." Pp. 117-139 in *Theories of Women's Studies*, edited by Gloria Bowles and Renate Duelli Klein. London: Routledge and Kegan Paul.

Milner, Allison, Rod McClure, Jing Sun, Diego De Leo. 2011. "Globalisation and Suicide: An empirical investigation in 35 countries over the period 1980-2006." *Health and Place* 17: 996-1003.

Modood, Tariq. 1997. "Culture and Identity." Pp. 290-338 in *Ethnic Minorities in Britain*, edited by Tariq Modood and Richard Berthoud. London: Policy Studies Institute.

—. 2007. *Multiculturalism*. Cambridge: Polity.

Mol, Hans. 1976. *Identity and the Sacred*. Oxford: Basil Blackwell.

—, ed. 1978. *Identity and Religion*. London: Sage Publications.

Morrison, Karl F. 1992. *Understanding Conversion*: London.

Moughrabi, Fouad M. 1978. "The Arab Basic Personality: A Critical Survey of the Literature." *International Journal of Middle East Studies* 9: 99-112.

Moussalli, Ahmad S. 1998. "Islamic Fundamentalist Perceptions of Other Monotheistic Religions." in *Islam and Christianity: Mutual Perceptions since the mid-twentieth Century*, edited by Jacques Waardenburg. Leuven, Switzernland: Peeters.

Myers, Scott M. 1996. "`An Interactive Model of Religiosity Inheritance: The Importance of Family Context." *American Sociological Review* 61: 858-866.

Nahle, Rania Ahmed. 1996. "Islam and Women's Human Rights: A Reapprisal in Light of the Qur'an and the Hadith." *Al-Raida* XIII: 45-48.

Paper, Jordan. 1999. "Conversion from Within and Without in Chinese Religion." Pp. 102-114 in *Religious Conversion: Contemporary Practices and Controversies*, edited by Christopher Lamb and M. Darrol Bryant. London: Cassell.

Parshall, Phil. 1980. *New Paths in Muslim Evangelism*. Grand Rapids, MI: Baker Book House.

—. 1999. "Going Too Far." Pp. 655-657 in *Perspectives on the World Christian Movement: A Reader*, edited by Ralph D. Winter and Steven C. Hawthorne. Pasadena, CA: William Carey Library.

Pease, Bob. 2012. "Interrogating Privileged Subjectivities: Reflections on Writing Personal Accounts of Privilege." in *Emergent Writing Methodologies in Feminist Studies*, edited by Livholts, Mona. London: Routledge.

Peristiany, J.G., ed. 1965. *Honour and Shame*. London: Weidenfeld and Nicolson.

Ponticelli, Christy M. 1999. "Crafting Stories of Sexual Identity Reconstruction." *Social Psychology Quarterly* 62: 157-172.

Radcliffe-Brown, Alfred. 1974. "excerpt from "Religion and Society"." Pp. 588-605 in *Classical Approaches to the Study of Religion*, edited by Jacques Waardenburg. Paris: Walter de Gruyter.

Rahman, S. A. 1996. *Punishment of Apostasy in Islam*. New Delhi: Kitab Bhavan.

Rambo, Lewis R. 1993. *Understanding Religious Conversion*. London: Yale University Press.

—. 1999. "Theories of Conversion: Understanding and Interpreting Religious Change." *Social Compass* 46: 259-271.

Rambo, Lewis R., and Charles A. Farhadian. 1999. "Converting: Stages of Religious Change." Pp. 23-34 in *Religious Conversion: Contemporary Practices and Controversies*, edited by Christopher Lamb and M. Darrol Bryant. London: Cassell.

Reisacher, Evelyne. 2005. "North African Women and Conversion: Specifics of Female Faith and Experience." Pp. 109-123 in *From the Straight Path to the Narrow Way*, edited by David H. Greenlee. Milton Keynes, Bucks: Authentic.

Reiss, Steven. 2000. "Why People Turn to Religion: A Motivational Analysis." *Journal for the Scientific Study of Religion* 39: 47-52.

Renzetti, Claire M., and Raymond M. Lee, eds. 1993. *Researching Sensitive Topics*. London: Sage Publications.

Ribner, David S., and Ruben Schindler. 1996. "The Crisis of Religious Identity among Ethiopian Immigrants in Israel." *Journal of Black Studies* 27: 104-117.

Richardson, James T. 1985. "The Active vs. Passive Convert: Paradigm Conflict in Conversion/Recruitment Research." *Journal for the Scientific Study of Religion* 24: 163-179.

Riessman, Catherine Kohler. 2002. "Doing Justice: Positioning the Interpreter in Narrative Work." Pp. 193-211 in *Strategic Narrative: New Perspectives on the Power of Personal and Cultural Stories*, edited by Wendy Patterson. Oxford: Lexington Books.

Roald, Anne Sofie. 2006. "The Shaping of a Scandinavian Islam." Pp. 48-70 in *Women Embracing Islam*, edited by Karin van Nieuwkerk. Austin: University of Texas Press.

Robertson, Roland. 1970. *The Sociological Interpretation of Religion*. Oxford: Basil Blackwell.

—. 1992. *Globalization: Social Theory and Global Culture*. London: Sage Publications.

Rose, Gordon. 1966. "Anomie and Deviation -- A Conceptual Framework for Empirical Studies." *The British Journal of Sociology* 17: 29-45.

Rothbaum, Susan. 1988. "Between Two Worlds: Issues of Separation and Identity After Leaving a Religious Community." Pp. 205-228 in *Falling From the Faith: Causes and Consequences of Religious Apostasy*, edited by David G. Bromley. London: Sage Publications.

Roy, Olivier. 2004. *Globalised Islam: The Search for a New Umma*. London: Hurst and Company.

Ruthven, Malise. 1990. *A Satanic Affair*. London: Chatto and Windus.

Rynkiewich, Michael A., and James P. Spradley. 1976. *Ethics and Anthropology: Dilemmas in Fieldwork*. London: John Wiley and Sons.

Saadawi, Nawal El. 1980. *The Hidden Face of Eve*. London: Zed Books Ltd.

Saeed, Abdullah, and Hassan Saeed. 2004. *Freedom of Religion, Apostasy and Islam*. Burlington, VT: Ashgate.

Sahas, Daniel J. 1991. "The Seventh Century in Byzantine-Muslim Relations: Characteristics and Forces." *Islam and Christian-Muslim Relations* 2: 4-17.

Sahr, Monika Wohlrab. 2006. "Symbolizing Distance: Conversion to Islam in Germany." Pp. 71-92 in *Women Embracing Islam*, edited by Karin van Nieuwkerk. Austin: University of Texas Press.

Sardar, Ziauudin. 1991. "The Ethical Connection: Christian-Muslim Relations in the Postmodern Age." *Islam and Christian-Muslim Relations* 2: 56-76.

Schwartz, Seth J., Koen Luyckx, Vivian L. Vignoles. 2011. *Handbook of Identity Theory and Research*, vol. 1. London: Springer.

Sennett, Richard. 1998. *The Corrosion of Character*. London: W. W. Norton and Company.

Shanahan, Rodger. 2005. *The Shi'a of Lebanon: Clans, Parties and Clerics*. London: Tauris Academic Studies.

Shankland, David. 1999. *Islam and Society in Turkey*. Huntingdon, Cambridgeshire: The Eothen Press.

Shboul, Ahmad M.H. 1999. "Arab-Islamic Perceptions of Byzantine Religion and Culture." Pp. 122-135 in *Muslim Perceptions of Other Religions*, edited by Jacques Waardenburg. Oxford: Oxford University Press.

Shoham, S. Giora. 1976. *Social Deviance*. London: Gardner Press Inc.

Sikand, Yoginder S. 1999. "Women and the Tablighi Jama'at." *Islam and Christian-Muslim Relations* 10: 41-52.

Singerman, Diane. 1995. *Avenues of Participation: Family, Politics, and Networks in Urban Quarters of Cairo*. Princeton: Princeton University Press.

Slaughter, M.M. 1993. "The Salman Rushdie Affair: Apostasy, Honor, and Freedom of Speech." *Virginia Law Review* 79: 141-198.

Smilde, David. 2007. *Reason to Believe: Cultural Agency in Latin American Evangelicalism*. London: University of California Press.

Smith, Dorothy E. 1990. *Texts, Facts, and Femininity*. London: Routledge.

Smith, Jackie and Tina Fetner. "Structural Approaches in the Sociology of Social Movements." in *Handbook of Social Movements Across Disciplines*, edited by Bert Klandermans and Conny Roggeband, eds. 2007. New York: Springer.

Smith, Linda Tuhiwai. 1999. *Decolonizing Methodologies*. London: Zed Books.

Snow, David A., and Richard Machalek. 1984. "The Sociology of Conversion." *Annual Review of Sociology* 10: 167-190.

Sommer, Annie Van, and Samuel M. Zwemer. 1907. *Our Moslem Sisters*. London: Fleming H. Revell Company.

Sontag, Susan. 1966. *Against Interpretation and Other Essays*. New York: Farrar, Strauss and Giroux.

Spinner-Halev, Jeff, and Elizabeth Theiss-Morse. 2003. "National Identity and Self-Esteem." *Perspectives on Politics* 1: 515-532.

Sremac, Srdan. 2010. "Converting into a New Reality: Social Constructionism, Practical Theology and Conversion." *Nova Prisutnost* 8: 7-27.

Stanley, Gordon. 1964. "Personality and Attitude Correlates of Religious Conversion." *Journal for the Scientific Study of Religion* 4: 60-63.

Staples, Clifford L., and Armand L. Mauss. 1987. "Conversion or Commitment? A Reassessment of the Snow and Machalek Approach to the Study of Conversion." *Journal for the Scientific Study of Religion* 26: 133-147.

Stark, Rodney. 1973. "Age and Faith: A Changing Outlook." Pp. 48-57 in *Religion in Sociological Perspective: Essays in the Empirical Study of Religion*, edited by Charles Y. Glock. Belmont, CA: Wadsworth Publishing Co.

Stark, Rodney, and William Sims Bainbridge. 1985. *The Future of Religion*. London: University of California Press.

—. 1996. *Religion, Deviance, and Social Control*. London: Routledge.

Stark, Rodney, and Roger Finke. 2000. *Acts of Faith*. London: University of California Press.

Stryker, Sheldon. 1987. "The Vitalization of Symbolic Interactionism." *Social Psychology Quarterly* 50: 83-94.

Stryker, Sheldon, and Richard T. Serpe. 1994. "Identity Salience and Psychological Centrality: Equivalent, Overlapping, or Complementary Concepts?" *Social Psychology Quarterly* 57: 16-35.

Sumner, Colin. 1994. *The Sociology of Deviance: An Obituary*. Buckingham: Open University Press.

Sutcliffe, Sally. 1997. *Aisha My Sister*. Carlisle, Cumbria: Solway.

Syrjänen, Seppo. 1987. *In Search of Meaning and Identity: Conversion to Christianity in Pakistani Muslim Culture*. Vammala: The Finnish Society for Missiology and Ecumenics.

Tamadonfar, Mehran. 2001. "Islam, Law, and Political Control in Contemporary Iran." *Journal for the Scientific Study of Religion* 40: 205-220.

Tawney, R. H. 1938. *Religion and the Rise of Capitalism*. Middlesex: Pelican Books.

Taylor, Donald. 1999. "Conversion: inward, outward and awkward." Pp. 35-50 in *Religious Conversion: Contemporary Practices and Controversies*, edited by Christopher Lamb and M. Darrol Bryant. London: Cassell.

Tessler, Mark A. 1978. "The Identity of Religious Minorities in Non-Secular States: Jews in Tunisia and Morocco and Arabs in Israel." *Comparative Studies in Society and History* 20: 359-373.

Tottoli, Roberto. 2002. *Biblical Prophets in the Qu'ran and Muslim Literature*. Richmond, Surrey: Curzon Press.

Towler, Robert. 1974. *Homoreligiosus: Sociological Problems in the Study of Religion*. London: Constable.

Travis, John. 1999. "The C1 to C6 Spectrum." Pp. 658-659 in *Perspectives on the World Christian Movement: A Reader*, edited by Ralph D. Winter and Steven C. Hawthorne. Pasadena, CA: William Carey Library.

—. 1999. "Must all Muslims Leave 'Islam' to Follow Jesus?" Pp. 660-663 in *Perspectives on the World Christian Movement: A Reader*, edited by Ralph D. Winter and Steven C. Hawthorne. Pasadena, CA: William Carey Library.

—. 2000. "Messianic Muslim Followers of Isa: A Closer Look at C5 Believers and Congregations." *International Journal of Frontier Missions* 17: 53-59.

Travisano, R. 1970. "Alteration and conversion as qualitatively different transformations." Pp. 594-606 in *Social Psychology Through Symbolic Interactionism*, edited by G.P. Stone and H. Faberman. Waltham, Mass: Ginn-Blaisdell.

Tucker, Ruth. 1983. *From Jerusalem to Irian Jaya: A Biographical History of Christian Missions*. Grand Rapids, MI: Zondervan.

Vahiduddin, Syed. 1990. "Islam and Diversity of Religions." *Islam and Christian-Muslim Relations* 1: 3-11.

van Nieuwkerk, Karin. 2006. "Gender, Conversion and Islam: A Comparison of Online and Offline Conversion Narratives." Pp. 95-119 in *Women Embracing Islam*, edited by Karin van Nieuwkerk. Austin: University of Texas Press.

—, ed. 2006. *Women Embracing Islam*. Austin: University of Texas Press.

Verkuyten, Maykel. 2011. "Religious Identity and Socio-Religious Participation: Muslim Minorities in Western Europe." in *Identity and Participation in Culturally Diverse Societies*, edited by Assaad Azzi, Xenia Chryssochoou, Bert Klandermans and Bernard Simon. Oxford: Blackwell.

Waetjen, Herman C. 2001. "The Subversion of 'World' by the Parable of the Friend at Midnight." *Journal of Biblical Literature* 120: 703-721.

Warraq, Ibn. 2003. *Why I am Not a Muslim*. Amherst, NY: Prometheus Books.

Warraq, Ibn, ed. 2003. *Leaving Islam*. New York: Prometheus Books.

Watenpaugh, Keith David. 2006. *Being Modern in the Middle East*. Oxford: Princeton University Press.

Watt, W. Montgomery. 1961. *Islam and the Integration of Society*. London: Routledge & Kegan Paul.

—. 1995. *The Faith and Practice of Al-Ghazali*. Oxford: Oneworld Publications.

Weber, Max. 1968. *The Protestant Ethic and the Spirit of Capitalism*. London: Unwin University Books.

—. 1991. *The Sociology of Religion*. Boston: Beacon Press.

Weiner, Justus R. 1999. "Human Rights Trends in the Emerging Palestinian State: Problems Encountered by Muslim Converts to Christianity." *Detroit College of Law Journal of International Law* 539-594.

Werbner, Pnina. 1996. "Allegories of Sacred Imperfection: Magic, Hermeneutics, and Passion in the Satanic Verses." *Current Anthropology* 37: S55-S86.

—. 2002. *Imagined Diasporas Among Manchester Muslims*. Oxford: James Currey.

Williamson, Lori. 1999. "Women's History and Biography." *Gender and History* 11: 379-384.

Woodberry, J. Dudley, ed. 1989. *Muslims and Christians on the Emmaus Road*. Pasadena, CA: MARC.

—. 2005. "A Global Perspective on Muslims Coming to Faith in Christ." Pp. 11-22 in *From the Straight Path to the Narrow Way*, edited by David H. Greenlee. Milton Keynes, Bucks: Authentic.

Yang, Fenggang. 1999. *Chinese Christians in America*. University Park, PA: The Pennsylvania State University Press.

Yang, Fenggang, and Helen Rose Ebaugh. 2001. "Religion and Ethnicity Among New Immigrants: The Impact of Majority/Minority Status in Home and Host Countries." *Journal for the Scientific Study of Religion* 40: 364-378.

Yang, Fenggang, and Joseph B. Tamney. 2006. "Exploring Mass Conversion to Christianity Among the Chinese: An Introduction." *Sociology of Religion* 67: 125-129.

Yates, Timothy. 2000. "Christian Conversion 1900-2000: William James to Lewis Rambo." Pp. 124-138 in *Previous Convictions*, edited by Martyn Percy. London: SPCK.

Youssef, Nadia. 1973. "Cultural Ideals, Feminine Behavior and Family Control." *Comparative Studies in Society and History* 15: 326-347.

Zaidi, Ali. 2011. *Islam, Modernity, and the Human Sciences*. New York: Palgrave MacMillan.

Zajda, Joseph. 2011. "Globalisation and schooling: equity and access issues." *Cultural Studies of Science Education* 6: 143-152.

Zebiri, Kate. 1997. *Muslims and Christians Face to Face*. Oxford: Oneworld Publications.

—. 2001. "Muslim Perceptions of Christianity and the West." in *Islamic Interpretations of Christianity*, edited by Lloyd Ridgeon. Surrey: Curzon Press.

Zeid, Abou A.M. 1965. "Honour and Shame among the Bedouins of Egypt." Pp. 243-259 in *Honour and Shame*, edited by J.G. Peristiany. London: Weidenfeld and Nicolson.

Zinnbauer, Brian J., and Kenneth I. Pargament. 1998. "Spiritual Conversion: A Study of Religious Change among College Students." *Journal for the Scientific Study of Religion* 37: 161-180.

Zubaida, Sami. 1995. "Is there a Muslim Society? Ernest Gellner's Sociology of Islam" *Economy and Society* 24:151-188

—. 2003. *Law and Power in the Islamic World*. London: I.B. Tauris.

—. 2009. *Islam, the People and the State: Political Ideas and Movements in the Middle East*, 3rd ed. London: I.B. Taurus.

—. 2011. *Beyond Islam: A New Understanding of the Middle East.* London: I.B. Taurus.

Index

advocacy, 27
affiliation, 6, 8, 11, 63, 64, 99, 103, 109, 110
Allah, 36
America, 48, 64, 68, 117
apostasy, 6, 8, 11, 53, 54, 55, 75, 86, 87, 88, 91, 92, 101, 115
apostate, 2, 54, 61, 92, 94, 106
Arab, i, 3, 5, 9, 2, 8, 10, 11, 12, 13, 14, 15, 16, 19, 20, 21, 22, 23, 24, 25, 26, 35, 37, 38, 39, 42, 44, 45, 48, 49, 50, 53, 54, 56, 57, 58, 63, 64, 65, 66, 70, 71, 72, 73, 76, 77, 79, 80, 82, 83, 84, 86, 87, 88, 92, 94, 95, 97, 100, 101, 103, 105, 108, 111, 117, 118, 120
Armstrong (Karen), 37, 39, 40, 47, 90
assimilation, 104
attachment, 9, 99
attribution scheme, 66, 67
belief, 3, 39, 40, 41, 42, 43, 47, 50, 52, 53, 54, 55, 56, 58, 65, 85, 94, 99, 102, 112
believer, 1, 32, 36, 39, 41, 44, 52, 59, 69, 71, 82, 85, 95, 113, 119
belonging, 26, 56, 82, 83, 97, 99, 100
betray, 32
bias, 4, 24, 82, 84, 120
Bible, 3, 9, 30, 35, 61, 64, 67, 81, 90, 112, 113, 114, 117
biographical reconstruction, 66
bitterness, 81
blame, 86
blasphemy, 6, 53
Byzantine, 64
Camel Method, 35
Catholic, 8, 107, 111
chat, 10, 13
Chinese, 104, 105, 132
Christian, 2, 1, 2, 3, 5, 6, 7, 8, 9, 10, 11, 12, 15, 21, 23, 24, 26, 27, 33, 35, 38, 42, 43, 44, 45, 47, 48, 50, 52, 55, 56, 57, 58, 60, 61, 63, 64, 65, 67, 68, 69, 70, 71, 73, 75, 76, 77, 79, 80, 81, 82, 83, 84, 85, 87, 88, 90, 91, 92, 93, 94, 95, 97, 100, 101, 102, 103, 104, 105, 106, 107, 108, 109, 110, 111, 112, 113, 114, 115, 116, 117, 118, 119, 120, 121
Christianity, 2, 8, 2, 5, 7, 8, 9, 16, 26, 35, 42, 44, 45, 52, 56, 58, 63, 64, 65, 66, 67, 68, 71, 73, 76, 81, 82, 84, 86, 87, 88, 92, 94, 95, 100, 101, 102, 104, 105, 106, 107, 108, 109, 110, 113, 114, 115, 116, 117, 118, 119
church, 4, 9, 21, 23, 43, 51, 52, 56, 57, 59, 60, 61, 63, 64, 65, 67, 68, 77, 82, 83, 84, 85, 91, 94, 104, 105, 107, 109, 112, 114, 116, 117, 118, 120
circles, 11, 12, 24, 37, 40, 45, 56, 88, 89, 97, 112, 121
code, 86
communal, 11, 35, 40, 48, 51, 55, 76, 79
communist, 54, 64
concealment, 88
contextualisation, 45, 101
co-producing fieldwork, 28
creed, 6, 36, 38, 39, 40, 54, 55, 99, 100, 102
Crusades, 64
deceit, 93
democracy, 53
depression, 90
deviant, 8, 22, 51, 74, 81, 87, 88, 90, 91, 101, 104, 121
diaspora, 10
discredit, 93
discreditable, 88, 89, 90, 91, 92, 95
discredited, 88, 89, 90, 92
disillusionment, 7
diversity, 38, 54, 72, 79, 111

division, 79
Do No Harm, 8, 71, 73, 123
education, 9, 12, 42, 61, 116, 118, 119
Egypt, 10, 11, 12, 13, 14, 15, 24, 29, 38, 53, 56, 63, 108, 118
employment, 9, 67, 70, 73, 90
Enlightenment, 49, 65
enthusiasm, 75, 76, 81, 112
Europe, 3, 5, 48, 54, 56, 64, 65, 70, 77, 98, 117
expectation, 29, 30, 31, 42, 50, 51, 58, 67, 74, 75, 94, 99, 110
family, 1, 2, 7, 9, 10, 12, 21, 23, 31, 38, 40, 43, 47, 48, 50, 51, 55, 60, 61, 62, 63, 64, 66, 67, 68, 69, 71, 72, 74, 75, 76, 78, 79, 80, 82, 83, 85, 86, 87, 88, 89, 90, 91, 92, 93, 94, 95, 99, 100, 102, 103, 107, 113, 114, 116, 117, 118, 119, 120, 121
follower, 5, 107, 109
foreigner, 13, 20, 21, 23, 24, 58, 72, 89
fragmentary, 105, 108, 109, 117
friendship, 9, 14, 28, 30, 31, 57, 59, 61
frustration, 22, 59, 63, 68, 70, 73, 74, 77, 78, 83
fundamentalist, 52
fusive, 77, 105, 106, 107, 111, 117
gatekeeper, 15, 43
Gaudeul (Jean-Marie), 38, 83, 127
God, 32, 36, 39, 43, 44, 50, 51, 55, 65, 69, 72, 75, 77, 83, 93, 95, 108, 109
government, 11, 12, 14, 41, 42, 53, 70, 117
hadith, 54
harassment, 69, 119
hierarchy, 82
hijab, 35, 42, 61
history, 7, 23, 26, 35, 36, 37, 38, 39, 40, 48, 63, 64, 66, 73, 83, 94, 100, 102, 107, 117
homosexuality, 88, 91
honour, 2, 6, 29, 80, 85, 86, 87, 88, 91, 92, 93, 94, 100
honour killing, 86, 92
honourable, 69, 80, 85, 86, 94, 95, 110
human rights, 12, 55
humanitarian, 72
idealism, idealistic, idealised, 74, 77
identities, 14, 25, 27, 71, 74, 79, 82, 97, 100, 102, 103, 104, 105, 106, 108, 109, 110, 111, 116, 117, 118, 119
identity, 2, 5, 6, 12, 16, 17, 24, 26, 28, 35, 37, 38, 39, 45, 49, 50, 52, 55, 56, 60, 63, 66, 67, 73, 75, 77, 80, 84, 85, 86, 87, 88, 89, 90, 91, 92, 93, 94, 95, 97, 98, 99, 100, 101, 102, 103, 104, 105, 106, 107, 108, 109, 110, 111, 112, 113, 114, 115, 116, 117, 118, 119, 120, 121
ignore, 54, 55, 74, 77, 91, 92, 93
ijtihad, 40
immigrant, immigration, 69, 104
individual, individualism, individuality, 6, 7, 9, 11, 13, 21, 25, 29, 33, 36, 38, 40, 44, 49, 50, 51, 52, 53, 54, 55, 59, 60, 66, 67, 68, 73, 74, 81, 86, 87, 88, 89, 90, 91, 92, 94, 97, 98, 99, 100, 102, 119, 120
informant, 72
informed consent, 16, 30, 31
insider, 20, 21, 24, 26, 28
Insider Movement, 101, 103, 106
integration (types of identity integration), 20, 76, 77, 105, 106, 107, 108, 109, 111, 117
Internet, 10, 29
Isa, 3
Islam, 1, 3, 6, 7, 8, 10, 11, 12, 13, 14, 21, 26, 33, 35, 36, 37, 38, 39, 40, 41, 42, 43, 44, 47, 48, 49, 50, 51, 52, 53, 54, 55, 56, 57, 58, 61, 64, 65, 66, 67, 68, 76, 78, 81, 82, 83, 84, 86, 87, 88, 92, 93, 95, 100, 101, 102, 104, 105, 106, 107, 108, 113, 114, 115, 116, 117, 118, 119, 120, 121
Islamic, Islamic law, 2, 8, 12, 16, 35, 37, 38, 40, 42, 45, 47, 48, 49, 51, 52, 53, 54, 64, 100, 102, 108
Islamist, 42, 53, 128
Jesus, Christ, 2, 3, 5, 9, 10, 30, 35, 45, 56, 58, 59, 63, 64, 65, 67, 68, 69, 84, 87, 93, 94, 97, 101, 106, 107, 109, 116, 119, 120
jihad, 41
jurisdiction, 54
Khaldun (Ibn), 40, 41, 50
kinship, 48
label, 85, 89, 90, 97, 109, 110, 111, 120

language, 6, 15, 93, 110, 113
law, 38, 53, 54, 60, 102, 119
Lebanon, Lebanese, 9, 10, 11, 12, 13, 14, 15, 24, 29, 35, 38, 56, 63, 64, 68, 108, 118
legal, legally, 8, 12, 14, 48, 54, 58, 60, 69, 74, 84, 92, 101, 106, 108, 115, 117, 118
loneliness, lonely, 2, 76
majority, 6, 10, 11, 15, 25, 26, 40, 52, 84, 116
marriage, marry, married, 5, 8, 12, 14, 31, 39, 44, 60, 61, 62, 77, 81, 83, 91, 94, 107
MBB (Muslim-Background Believer), 5, 15, 19, 21, 22, 24, 33, 60, 61, 62, 84, 105, 109, 111, 116, 118
Mecca, 36, 40, 48, 50
Medina, 40, 48
men, man, 60, 125, 126, 131
mentor, 59, 111
Mernissi (Fatima), 35, 36, 49, 50, 51, 53, 54, 55
Middle East, 3, 10, 13, 15, 20, 21, 23, 26, 29, 37, 38, 40, 44, 45, 50, 56, 59, 63, 64, 65, 66, 68, 70, 75, 79, 80, 88, 90, 103, 104, 107, 108, 114, 117
minority, 10, 11, 19, 25, 26, 44, 57, 58, 64, 80, 84, 85, 99
miracle, 9
missiology, missiologist, missiological, 2, 35, 45, 97, 111
missionary, missionaries, 9, 11, 12, 14, 15, 20, 23, 26, 44, 45, 56, 58, 59, 61, 65, 69, 70, 71, 72, 73, 77, 78, 81, 101, 111, 112, 121
modernity, modern, 41, 49, 51, 65
money, 59, 68, 69, 70, 71
moral, morally, 4, 32, 73, 74, 76
Morocco, Moroccan, 10, 35, 103, 108, 118
movement, 10, 12, 13, 27, 39, 42, 49, 53, 54, 65, 73, 84, 90
Muhammad, 36, 37, 38, 39, 40, 48, 51, 92
Muslim, 5, 2, 3, 5, 6, 7, 8, 9, 10, 11, 12, 15, 16, 21, 25, 27, 31, 35, 36, 37, 38, 39, 40, 41, 42, 43, 44, 47, 48, 49, 50, 51, 52, 53, 54, 55, 56, 57, 58, 59, 60, 61, 63, 64, 65, 66, 67, 69, 71, 73, 75, 76, 77, 79, 80, 81, 82, 84, 87, 88, 91, 92, 93, 97, 100, 101, 102, 103, 104, 105, 106, 107, 108, 109, 110, 111, 113, 114, 115, 116, 117, 118, 119, 120, 121
Muslim-Christian relations (or Christian-Muslim relations), 64, 66
mutanasrin, 9, 2, 105, 108, 109
narrative research, 13, 28
nationalist, 39, 53
neglect, 30
nomad, nomadic, 51
North Africa, 10, 85, 108, 117, 118
on-line (online), 10, 13, 15, 69, 71
optimism, 73
Orthodox, 9, 44, 107, 111, 113
other, 9, 1, 2, 7, 8, 9, 10, 11, 12, 13, 14, 15, 19, 20, 21, 22, 23, 24, 25, 26, 28, 29, 30, 33, 36, 37, 41, 42, 43, 44, 47, 48, 49, 51, 52, 55, 56, 57, 58, 59, 60, 61, 64, 65, 68, 69, 70, 71, 72, 73, 74, 77, 78, 79, 80, 81, 82, 84, 85, 86, 87, 88, 89, 90, 91, 92, 94, 95, 97, 98, 99, 102, 104, 106, 108, 109, 110, 111, 112, 113, 114, 116, 117, 118, 120, 121
outsider, 20, 21, 22, 25, 26, 83, 89, 107
partner (life partner), 56, 60
polarisation, 63, 100
political Islam, 52
politics, polity, political, 11, 13, 15, 20, 36, 38, 40, 41, 42, 47, 48, 49, 52, 54, 57, 64, 65, 66, 71, 102, 106
power, 11, 23, 24, 27, 41, 52, 64, 65, 78, 121
practices, 4, 14, 35, 37, 38, 39, 40, 42, 43, 50, 93, 104, 105, 113, 117
prayer, praying, pray, 1, 21, 39, 40, 42, 45, 68, 82, 83, 107, 113, 114
privilege, 9, 22
profane, 43, 44
Protestant, 11, 44, 55, 59, 107, 136
psychology, psychological, psychologist, 74, 89, 90, 101, 110, 116
radio, 9, 112
Ramadan, 40, 43, 45, 113, 114
rebellion, rebel, 51, 87, 94, 118, 119
reflexivity, 20, 22, 25
reject, rejection, 2, 3, 6, 43, 50, 53, 88, 89, 95, 100, 101, 112

relationship, relationships, 5, 6, 7, 8, 9, 10, 11, 14, 16, 19, 20, 21, 22, 23, 27, 28, 29, 30, 31, 32, 40, 43, 55, 56, 57, 58, 60, 61, 62, 63, 64, 71, 72, 73, 75, 76, 77, 79, 83, 84, 85, 87, 89, 90, 91, 94, 95, 98, 111, 112, 113, 119
reputation, 6, 61, 80, 85
researcher, 7, 19, 20, 22, 23, 24, 25, 26, 28, 29, 30, 31, 32, 33, 89
respect, 5, 14, 29, 32, 37, 52, 57, 58, 65, 67, 80, 82, 85, 93, 94, 95, 113
rights, 4, 3, 26, 35, 49, 51, 59
risk, 25, 69, 71, 72, 73, 79, 82, 90, 95, 101, 106, 118, 121
ritual, 40, 76, 82, 94, 99
role, 4, 8, 16, 20, 28, 29, 37, 39, 41, 43, 47, 59, 60, 64, 67, 79, 82, 83, 84, 87, 98, 104, 105, 113
rule, rules, 8, 38, 51, 54, 64, 65, 68, 74, 83, 86, 92, 109, 115
Rushdie (Salman Rushdie, Rushdie Affair), 6, 48
sacrament, 93
sacred, 4, 5, 6, 43, 44
sacrificial, sacrifice, 49, 71, 80
school, 27, 54, 67, 68, 70, 71, 84, 95, 116, 118
secret, 8, 16, 57, 72, 87, 88, 89, 90, 103
sectarian, 11, 36, 79
secular, 37, 40, 41, 48, 118
Secularism, secularist, 52, 53
sexually stigmatised, sexual stigma, 89, 90
shame, 6, 43, 48, 49, 55, 85, 86, 87, 88, 90, 91, 93, 94, 95
shirk, 36
shrine, 65
society, 4, 7, 22, 26, 35, 36, 37, 40, 41, 42, 47, 48, 50, 51, 53, 62, 63, 66, 71, 74, 76, 85, 86, 87, 88, 92, 94, 98, 99, 100, 101, 102, 103, 107, 108, 111, 112, 118, 121
spiritual, spiritually, 9, 6, 7, 9, 14, 41, 69, 92, 118
sponsor, sponsoring, 69
stigma, stigmatised, stigmatised, 19, 25, 27, 87, 88, 89, 90, 91, 101, 111
stress, 28, 61, 78, 89, 95, 110, 119
structure, 4, 8, 11, 25, 48, 74, 76, 86, 111, 113, 114, 121
Sufi, 39
sunna, 35, 37
Sunni, 10, 11, 39, 40, 54, 67, 106
suspicion, suspect, suspicious, 15, 20, 21, 33, 57, 63, 90, 92, 121
Symbolic Interactionism, symbolic interactionist, 83, 84
sympathiser, 24
syncretism, 105
tawhid, 16, 36, 38, 39, 42, 43, 44, 47, 48, 49, 51, 52, 53, 55, 58, 59, 60, 62, 68, 71, 76, 79, 92, 100, 101, 113
theology, theological, 2, 21, 35, 37, 44, 53, 54, 56, 64, 69, 79, 83, 94
tolerance, 51, 52, 53
trust, 11, 16, 19, 21, 24, 27, 31, 32, 33, 51, 57, 65, 71, 77, 81, 83, 84, 89, 121
Tunisia, Tunisian, 10, 108, 118, 135
umma, 16, 36, 40, 45, 47, 48, 49, 50, 51, 52, 53, 54, 55, 56, 57, 58, 59, 60, 61, 68, 70, 72, 73, 76, 82, 92, 99, 100, 103, 119
United Nations, 53
United States, 9, 3, 5, 56, 68, 70, 74, 77, 87, 98, 101, 104
unity, 16, 36, 37, 38, 40, 41, 42, 44, 47, 48, 49, 50, 51, 53, 79, 81, 82, 99, 101, 103, 107
Universal Declaration of Human Rights, 53, 54
universality, 40, 52
vulnerable, 19, 72, 119
waste, wasting, 59, 70
wealth, 59, 67, 68, 69, 74
West, Western, 8, 3, 11, 20, 23, 26, 41, 44, 47, 48, 49, 51, 52, 53, 55, 56, 59, 60, 65, 66, 67, 68, 69, 70, 71, 73, 76, 77, 87, 88, 98, 101, 102, 103, 105, 120
wise, 9, 21, 24, 89
women, woman, 5, 1, 2, 8, 9, 12, 14, 22, 23, 24, 25, 27, 31, 32, 35, 43, 44, 49, 51, 57, 59, 60, 61, 62, 67, 68, 69, 71, 72, 75, 77, 78, 79, 81, 82, 83, 86, 90, 91, 92, 93, 95, 105, 106, 107, 109, 112, 113, 117, 118
Yang (Fenggang), 9, 104, 105

REGNUM EDINBURGH 2010 SERIES
Series Listing

David A. Kerr, Kenneth R. Ross (Eds)
Mission Then and Now
2009 / 978-1-870345-73-6 / 343pp (paperback)
2009 / 978-1-870345-76-7 / 343pp (hardback)

No one can hope to fully understand the modern Christian missionary movement without engaging substantially with the World Missionary Conference, held at Edinburgh in 1910. This book is the first to systematically examine the eight Commissions which reported to Edinburgh 1910 and gave the conference much of its substance and enduring value. It will deepen and extend the reflection being stimulated by the upcoming centenary and will kindle the missionary imagination for 2010 and beyond.

Daryl M. Balia, Kirsteen Kim (Eds)
Witnessing to Christ Today
2010 / 978-1-870345-77-4 / 301pp

This volume, the second in the Edinburgh 2010 series, includes reports of the nine main study groups working on different themes for the celebration of the centenary of the World Missionary Conference, Edinburgh 1910. Their collaborative work brings together perspectives that are as inclusive as possible of contemporary world Christianity and helps readers to grasp what it means in different contexts to be 'witnessing to Christ today'.

Claudia Währisch-Oblau, Fidon Mwombeki (Eds)
Mission Continues
Global Impulses for the 21st Century
2010 / 978-1-870345-82-8 / 271pp

In May 2009, 35 theologians from Asia, Africa and Europe met in Wuppertal, Germany, for a consultation on mission theology organized by the United Evangelical Mission: Communion of 35 Churches in Three Continents. The aim was to participate in the 100th anniversary of the Edinburgh conference through a study process and reflect on the challenges for mission in the 21st century. This book brings together these papers written by experienced practitioners from around the world.

Brian Woolnough and Wonsuk Ma (Eds)
Holistic Mission
God's Plan for God's People
2010 / 978-1-870345-85-9 / 277pp

Holistic mission, or integral mission, implies God is concerned with the whole person, the whole community, body, mind and spirit. This book discusses the meaning of the holistic gospel, how it has developed, and implications for the church. It takes a global, eclectic approach, with 19 writers, all of whom have much experience in, and commitment to, holistic mission. It addresses critically and honestly one of the most exciting, and challenging, issues facing the church today. To be part of God's plan for God's people, the church must take holistic mission to the world.

Kirsteen Kim and Andrew Anderson (Eds)
Mission Today and Tomorrow
2010 / 978-1-870345-91-0 / 450pp

There are moments in our lives when we come to realise that we are participating in the triune God's mission. If we believe the church to be as sign and symbol of the reign of God in the world, then we are called to witness to Christ today by sharing in God's mission of love through the transforming power of the Holy Spirit. We can all participate in God's transforming and reconciling mission of love to the whole creation.

Tormod Engelsviken, Erling Lundeby and Dagfinn Solheim (Eds)
The Church Going Glocal
Mission and Globalisation
2011 / 978-1-870345-93-4 / 262pp

The New Testament church is… universal and local at the same time. The universal, one and holy apostolic church appears in local manifestations. Missiologically speaking… the church can take courage as she faces the increasing impact of globalisation on local communities today. Being universal and concrete, the church is geared for the simultaneous challenges of the glocal and local.

Marina Ngurusangzeli Behera (Ed)
Interfaith Relations after One Hundred Years
Christian Mission among Other Faiths
2011 / 978-1-870345-96-5 / 334pp

The essays of this book reflect not only the acceptance and celebration of pluralism within India but also by extension an acceptance as well as a need for unity among Indian Christians of different denominations. The essays were presented and studied at a preparatory consultation on Study Theme II: Christian Mission Among Other Faiths at the United Theological College, India July 2009.

Lalsangkima Pachuau and Knud Jørgensen (Eds)
Witnessing to Christ in a Pluralistic Age
Christian Mission among Other Faiths
2011 / 978-1-870345-95-8 / 277pp

In a world where plurality of faiths is increasingly becoming a norm of life, insights on the theology of religious plurality are needed to strengthen our understanding of our own faith and the faith of others. Even though religious diversity is not new, we are seeing an upsurge in interest on the theologies of religion among all Christian confessional traditions. It can be claimed that no other issue in Christian mission is more important and more difficult than the theologies of religions.

Beth Snodderly and A Scott Moreau (Eds)
Evangelical Frontier Mission
Perspectives on the Global Progress of the Gospel
2011 / 978-1-870345-98-9 / 312pp

This important volume demonstrates that 100 years after the World Missionary Conference in Edinburgh, Evangelism has become truly global. Twenty-first-century Evangelism continues to focus on frontier mission, but significantly, and in the spirit of Edinburgh 1910, it also has re-engaged social action.

Rolv Olsen (Ed)
Mission and Postmodernities
2011 / 978-1-870345-97-2 / 279pp

This volume takes on meaning because its authors honestly struggle with and debate how we should relate to postmodernities. Should our response be accommodation, relativizing or counter-culture? How do we strike a balance between listening and understanding, and at the same time exploring how postmodernities influence the interpretation and application of the Bible as the normative story of God's mission in the world?

Cathy Ross (Ed)
Life-Widening Mission
2012 / 978-1-908355-00-3 / 190pp

It is clear from the essays collected here that the experience of the 2010 World Mission Conference in Edinburgh was both affirming and frustrating for those taking part - affirming because of its recognition of how the centre of gravity has moved in global Christianity; frustrating because of the relative slowness of so many global Christian bodies to catch up with this and to embody it in the way they do business and in the way they represent themselves. These reflections will—or should—provide plenty of food for thought in the various councils of the Communion in the coming years.

Beate Fagerli, Knud Jørgensen, Rolv Olsen, Kari Storstein Haug and Knut Tveitereid (Eds)
A Learning Missional Church
Reflections from Young Missiologists
2012 / 978-1-908355-01-1 / 239pp

Cross-cultural mission has always been a primary learning experience for the church. It pulls us out of a mono-cultural understanding and helps us discover a legitimate theological pluralism which opens up for new perspectives in the Gospel. Translating the Gospel into new languages and cultures is a human and divine means of making us learn new 'incarnations' of the Good News.

REGNUM STUDIES IN GLOBAL CHRISTIANITY

(Previously GLOBAL THEOLOGICAL VOICES series)

Series Listing

David Emmanuel Singh (Ed)

Jesus and the Cross

Reflections of Christians from Islamic Contexts

2008 / 978-1-870345-65-1 / 226pp

The Cross reminds us that the sins of the world are not borne through the exercise of power but through Jesus Christ's submission to the will of the Father. The papers in this volume are organised in three parts: scriptural, contextual and theological. The central question being addressed is: how do Christians living in contexts, where Islam is a majority or minority religion, experience, express or think of the Cross?

Sung-wook Hong

Naming God in Korea

The Case of Protestant Christianity

2008 / 978-1-870345-66-8 / 170pp

Since Christianity was introduced to Korea more than a century ago, one of the most controversial issues has been the Korean term for the Christian 'God'. This issue is not merely about naming the Christian God in Korean language, but it relates to the question of theological contextualization - the relationship between the gospel and culture - and the question of Korean Christian identity. This book demonstrates the nature of the gospel in relation to cultures, i.e., the universality of the gospel expressed in all human cultures.

Hubert van Beek (Ed)

Revisioning Christian Unity

The Global Christian Forum

2009 / 978-1-870345-74-3 / 288pp

This book contains the records of the Global Christian Forum gathering held in Limuru near Nairobi, Kenya, on 6 – 9 November 2007 as well as the papers presented at that historic event. Also included are a summary of the Global Christian Forum process from its inception until the 2007 gathering and the reports of the evaluation of the process that was carried out in 2008.

Young-hoon Lee

The Holy Spirit Movement in Korea

Its Historical and Theological Development

2009 / 978-1-870345-67-5 / 174pp

This book traces the historical and theological development of the Holy Spirit Movement in Korea through six successive periods (from 1900 to the present time). These periods are characterized by repentance and revival (1900-20), persecution and suffering under Japanese occupation (1920-40), confusion and division (1940-60), explosive revival in which the Pentecostal movement played a major role in the rapid growth of Korean churches (1960-80), the movement reaching out to all denominations (1980-2000), and the new context demanding the Holy Spirit movement to open new horizons in its mission engagement (2000-).

Paul Hang-Sik Cho
Eschatology and Ecology
Experiences of the Korean Church
2010 / 978-1-870345-75-0 / 260pp

This book raises the question of why Korean people, and Korean Protestant Christians in particular, pay so little attention to ecological issues. The author argues that there is an important connection (or elective affinity) between this lack of attention and the other-worldly eschatology that is so dominant within Korean Protestant Christianity.

Dietrich Werner, David Esterline, Namsoon Kang, Joshva Raja (Eds)
The Handbook of Theological Education in World Christianity
Theological Perspectives, Ecumenical Trends, Regional Surveys
2010 / 978-1-870345-80-4 / 759pp

This major reference work is the first ever comprehensive study of Theological Education in Christianity of its kind. With contributions from over 90 international scholars and church leaders, it aims to be easily accessible across denominational, cultural, educational, and geographic boundaries. The Handbook will aid international dialogue and networking among theological educators, institutions, and agencies.

David Emmanuel Singh & Bernard C Farr (Eds)
Christianity and Education
Shaping of Christian Context in Thinking
2010 / 978-1-870345-81-1 / 374pp

Christianity and Education is a collection of papers published in *Transformation: An International Journal of Holistic Mission Studies* over a period of 15 years. The articles represent a spectrum of Christian thinking addressing issues of institutional development for theological education, theological studies in the context of global mission, contextually aware/informed education, and academies which deliver such education, methodologies and personal reflections.

David Emmanuel Singh (Ed)
Jesus and the Incarnation
Reflections of Christians from Islamic Contexts
2011 / 978-1-870345-90-3 / 250pp

In the dialogues of Christians with Muslims nothing is more fundamental than the Cross, the Incarnation and the Resurrection of Jesus. Building on the *Jesus and the Cross*, this book contains voices of Christians living in various 'Islamic contexts' and reflecting on the Incarnation of Jesus. The aim and hope of these reflections is that the papers weaved around the notion of 'the Word' will not only promote dialogue among Christians on the roles of the Person and the Book but, also, create a positive environment for their conversations with Muslim neighbours.

J.Andrew Kirk

Civilisations in Conflict?

Islam, the West and Christian Faith

2011 / 978-1-870345-87-3 / 205pp

Samuel Huntington's thesis, which argues that there appear to be aspects of Islam that could be on a collision course with the politics and values of Western societies, has provoked much controversy. The purpose of this study is to offer a particular response to Huntington's thesis by making a comparison between the origins of Islam and Christianity.

Ivan M Satyavrata

God Has Not left Himself Without Witness

2011 / 978-1-870345-79-8 / 260pp

Since its earliest inception the Christian Church has had to address the question of what common ground exits between Christian faiths and other religions. This issue is not merely of academic interest but one with critical existential and socio-political consequences. This study presents a case for the revitalization of the fulfillment tradition based on a recovery and assessment of the fulfillment approaches of Indian Christian converts in the pre-independence period.

REGNUM STUDIES IN MISSION
Series Listing

Kwame Bediako

Theology and Identity

The Impact of Culture upon Christian Thought in the Second Century and in Modern Africa

1992 / 978-1870345-10-1 / 508pp

The author examines the question of Christian identity in the context of the Graeco–Roman culture of the early Roman Empire. He then addresses the modern African predicament of quests for identity and integration.

Christopher Sugden

Seeking the Asian Face of Jesus

The Practice and Theology of Christian Social Witness in Indonesia and India 1974–1996

1997 / 1-870345-26-6 / 496pp

This study focuses on contemporary holistic mission with the poor in India and Indonesia combined with the call to transformation of all life in Christ with micro-credit enterprise schemes. 'The literature on contextual theology now has a new standard to rise to' – Lamin Sanneh (Yale University, USA).

Hwa Yung

Mangoes or Bananas?

The Quest for an Authentic Asian Christian Theology

1997 / 1-870345-25-5 / 274pp

Asian Christian thought remains largely captive to Greek dualism and Enlightenment rationalism because of the overwhelming dominance of Western culture. Authentic contextual Christian theologies will emerge within Asian Christianity with a dual recovery of confidence in culture and the gospel.

Keith E. Eitel

Paradigm Wars

The Southern Baptist International Mission Board Faces the Third Millennium

1999 / 1-870345-12-6 / 140pp

The International Mission Board of the Southern Baptist Convention is the largest denominational mission agency in North America. This volume chronicles the historic and contemporary forces that led to the IMB's recent extensive reorganization, providing the most comprehensive case study to date of a historic mission agency restructuring to continue its mission purpose into the twenty-first century more effectively.

Samuel Jayakumar

Dalit Consciousness and Christian Conversion

Historical Resources for a Contemporary Debate

1999 / 81-7214-497-0 / 434pp

(Published jointly with ISPCK)

The main focus of this historical study is social change and transformation among the Dalit Christian communities in India. Historiography tests the evidence in the light of the conclusions of the modern Dalit liberation theologians.

Vinay Samuel and Christopher Sugden (Eds)

Mission as Transformation

A Theology of the Whole Gospel

1999 / 978-18703455-13-2 / 522pp

This book brings together in one volume twenty five years of biblical reflection on mission practice with the poor from around the world. This volume helps anyone understand how evangelicals, struggling to unite evangelism and social action, found their way in the last twenty five years to the biblical view of mission in which God calls all human beings to love God and their neighbour; never creating a separation between the two.

Christopher Sugden

Gospel, Culture and Transformation

2000 / 1-870345-32-0 / 152pp

A Reprint, with a New Introduction,
of Part Two of Seeking the Asian Face of Jesus

Gospel, Culture and Transformation explores the practice of mission especially in relation to transforming cultures and communities. - 'Transformation is to enable God's vision of society to be actualised in all relationships: social, economic and spiritual, so that God's will may be reflected in human society and his love experienced by all communities, especially the poor.'

Bernhard Ott

Beyond Fragmentation: Integrating Mission and Theological Education

A Critical Assessment of some Recent Developments
in Evangelical Theological Education

2001 / 1-870345-14-2 / 382pp

Beyond Fragmentation is an enquiry into the development of Mission Studies in evangelical theological education in Germany and German-speaking Switzerland between 1960 and 1995. The author undertakes a detailed examination of the paradigm shifts which have taken place in recent years in both the theology of mission and the understanding of theological education.

Gideon Githiga

The Church as the Bulwark against Authoritarianism

Development of Church and State Relations in Kenya, with Particular Reference to the Years after Political Independence 1963-1992

2002 / 1-870345-38-x / 218pp

'All who care for love, peace and unity in Kenyan society will want to read this careful history by Bishop Githiga of how Kenyan Christians, drawing on the Bible, have sought to share the love of God, bring his peace and build up the unity of the nation, often in the face of great difficulties and opposition.' Canon Dr Chris Sugden, Oxford Centre for Mission Studies.

Myung Sung-Hoon, Hong Young-Gi (eds.)

Charis and Charisma

David Yonggi Cho and the Growth of Yoido Full Gospel Church

2003 / 978-1870345-45-3 / 218pp

This book discusses the factors responsible for the growth of the world's largest church. It expounds the role of the Holy Spirit, the leadership, prayer, preaching, cell groups and creativity in promoting church growth. It focuses on God's grace (charis) and inspiring leadership (charisma) as the two essential factors and the book's purpose is to present a model for church growth worldwide.

Samuel Jayakumar
Mission Reader
Historical Models for Wholistic Mission in the Indian Context
2003 / 1-870345-42-8 / 250pp
(Published jointly with ISPCK)

This book is written from an evangelical point of view revalidating and reaffirming the Christian commitment to wholistic mission. The roots of the 'wholistic mission' combining 'evangelism and social concerns' are to be located in the history and tradition of Christian evangelism in the past; and the civilizing purpose of evangelism is compatible with modernity as an instrument in nation building.

Bob Robinson
Christians Meeting Hindus
An Analysis and Theological Critique of the Hindu-Christian Encounter in India
2004 / 987-1870345-39-2 / 392pp

This book focuses on the Hindu-Christian encounter, especially the intentional meeting called dialogue, mainly during the last four decades of the twentieth century, and specifically in India itself.

Gene Early
Leadership Expectations
How Executive Expectations are Created and Used in a Non-Profit Setting
2005 / 1-870345-30-4 / 276pp

The author creates an Expectation Enactment Analysis to study the role of the Chancellor of the University of the Nations-Kona, Hawaii. This study is grounded in the field of managerial work, jobs, and behaviour and draws on symbolic interactionism, role theory, role identity theory and enactment theory. The result is a conceptual framework for developing an understanding of managerial roles.

Tharcisse Gatwa
The Churches and Ethnic Ideology in the Rwandan Crises 1900-1994
2005 / 978-1870345-24-8 / 300pp
(Reprinted 2011)

Since the early years of the twentieth century Christianity has become a new factor in Rwandan society. This book investigates the role Christian churches played in the formulation and development of the racial ideology that culminated in the 1994 genocide.

Julie Ma
Mission Possible
Biblical Strategies for Reaching the Lost
2005 / 978-1870345-37-1 / 142pp

This is a missiology book for the church which liberates missiology from the specialists for the benefit of every believer. It also serves as a textbook that is simple and friendly, and yet solid in biblical interpretation. This book links the biblical teaching to the actual and contemporary missiological settings with examples, making the Bible come alive to the reader.

Allan Anderson, Edmond Tang (Eds)
Asian and Pentecostal
The Charismatic Face of Christianity in Asia
2005 / 978-1870345-94-1 / 596pp
(Reprinted 2011)
(Published jointly with APTS Press)

This book provides a thematic discussion and pioneering case studies on the history and development of Pentecostal and Charismatic churches in the countries of South Asia, South East Asia and East Asia.

I. Mark Beaumont
Christology in Dialogue with Muslims
A Critical Analysis of Christian Presentations of Christ for Muslims from the Ninth and Twentieth Centuries
2005 / 978-1870345-46-0 / 228pp

This book analyses Christian presentations of Christ for Muslims in the most creative periods of Christian-Muslim dialogue, the first half of the ninth century and the second half of the twentieth century. In these two periods, Christians made serious attempts to present their faith in Christ in terms that take into account Muslim perceptions of him, with a view to bridging the gap between Muslim and Christian convictions.

Thomas Czövek,
Three Seasons of Charismatic Leadership
A Literary-Critical and Theological Interpretation of the Narrative of Saul, David and Solomon
2006 / 978-1870345-48-4 / 272pp

This book investigates the charismatic leadership of Saul, David and Solomon. It suggests that charismatic leaders emerge in crisis situations in order to resolve the crisis by the charisma granted by God. Czovek argues that Saul proved himself as a charismatic leader as long as he acted resolutely and independently from his mentor Samuel. In the author's eyes, Saul's failure to establish himself as a charismatic leader is caused by his inability to step out from Samuel's shadow.

Richard Burgess
Nigeria's Christian Revolution
The Civil War Revival and Its Pentecostal Progeny (1967-2006)
2008 / 978-1-870345-63-7 / 347pp

This book describes the revival that occurred among the Igbo people of Eastern Nigeria and the new Pentecostal churches it generated, and documents the changes that have occurred as the movement has responded to global flows and local demands. As such, it explores the nature of revivalist and Pentecostal experience, but does so against the backdrop of local socio-political and economic developments, such as decolonisation and civil war, as well as broader processes, such as modernisation and globalisation.

David Emmanuel Singh & Bernard C Farr (Eds)
Christianity and Cultures
Shaping Christian Thinking in Context
2008 / 978-1-870345-69-9 / 260pp

This volume marks an important milestone, the 25th anniversary of the Oxford Centre for Mission Studies (OCMS). The papers here have been exclusively sourced from Transformation, a quarterly journal of OCMS, and seek to provide a tripartite view of Christianity's engagement with cultures by focusing on the question: how is Christian thinking being formed or reformed through its interaction with the varied contexts it encounters? The subject matters include different strands of theological-missiological thinking, socio-political engagements and forms of family relationships in interaction with the host cultures.

Tormod Engelsviken, Ernst Harbakk, Rolv Olsen, Thor Strandenæs (Eds)
Mission to the World
Communicating the Gospel in the 21st Century:
Essays in Honour of Knud Jørgensen
2008 / 978-1-870345-64-4 / 472pp

Knud Jørgensen is Director of Areopagos and Associate Professor of Missiology at MF Norwegian School of Theology. This book reflects on the main areas of Jørgensen's commitment to mission. At the same time it focuses on the main frontier of mission, the world, the content of mission, the Gospel, the fact that the Gospel has to be communicated, and the context of contemporary mission in the 21st century.

Al Tizon
Transformation after Lausanne
Radical Evangelical Mission in Global-Local Perspective
2008 / 978-1-870345-68-2 / 281pp

After Lausanne '74, a worldwide network of radical evangelical mission theologians and practitioners use the notion of "Mission as Transformation" to integrate evangelism and social concern together, thus lifting theological voices from the Two Thirds World to places of prominence. This book documents the definitive gatherings, theological tensions, and social forces within and without evangelicalism that led up to Mission as Transformation. And it does so through a global-local grid that points the way toward greater holistic mission in the 21st century.

Bambang Budijanto
Values and Participation
Development in Rural Indonesia
2009 / 978-1-870345-70-4 / 237pp

Socio-religious values and socio-economic development are inter-dependant, inter-related and are constantly changing in the context of macro political structures, economic policy, religious organizations and globalization; and micro influences such as local affinities, identity, politics, leadership and beliefs. The book argues that the comprehensive approach in understanding the socio-religious values of each of the three local Lopait communities in Central Java is essential to accurately describing their respective identity.

Alan R. Johnson
Leadership in a Slum
A Bangkok Case Study
2009 / 978-1-870345-71-2 / 238pp

This book looks at leadership in the social context of a slum in Bangkok from a different perspective than traditional studies which measure well educated Thais on leadership scales derived in the West. Using both systematic data collection and participant observation, it develops a culturally preferred model as well as a set of models based in Thai concepts that reflect on-the-ground realities. It concludes by looking at the implications of the anthropological approach for those who are involved in leadership training in Thai settings and beyond.

Titre Ande
Leadership and Authority
Bula Matari and Life - Community Ecclesiology in Congo
2010 / 978-1-870345-72-9 / 189pp

Christian theology in Africa can make significant development if a critical understanding of the socio-political context in contemporary Africa is taken seriously, particularly as Africa's post-colonial Christian leadership based its understanding and use of authority on the Bula Matari model. This has caused many problems and Titre proposes a Life-Community ecclesiology for liberating authority, here leadership is a function, not a status, and 'apostolic succession' belongs to all people of God.

Frank Kwesi Adams
Odwira and the Gospel
A Study of the Asante Odwira Festival and its Significance for Christianity in Ghana
2010 /978-1-870345-59-0 / 232pp

The study of the Odwira festival is the key to the understanding of Asante religious and political life in Ghana. The book explores the nature of the Odwira festival longitudinally - in pre-colonial, colonial and post-independence Ghana - and examines the Odwira ideology and its implications for understanding the Asante self-identity. Also discussed is how some elements of faith portrayed in the

Odwira festival can provide a framework for Christianity to engage with Asante culture at a greater depth.

Bruce Carlton
Strategy Coordinator
Changing the Course of Southern Baptist Missions
2010 / 978-1-870345-78-1 / 268pp

This is an outstanding, one-of-a-kind work addressing the influence of the non-residential missionary/strategy coordinator's role in Southern Baptist missions. This scholarly text examines the twentieth century global missiological currents that influenced the leadership of the International Mission Board, resulting in a new paradigm to assist in taking the gospel to the nations.

Julie Ma & Wonsuk Ma
Mission in the Spirit:
Towards a Pentecostal/Charismatic Missiology
2010 / 978-1-870345-84-2 / 312pp

The book explores the unique contribution of Pentecostal/Charismatic mission from the beginning of the twentieth century. The first part considers the theological basis of Pentecostal/Charismatic mission thinking and practice. Special attention is paid to the Old Testament, which has been regularly overlooked by the modern Pentecostal/Charismatic movements. The second part discusses major mission topics with contributions and challenges unique to Pentecostal/Charismatic mission. The book concludes with a reflection on the future of this powerful missionary movement. As the authors served as Korean missionaries in Asia, often their missionary experiences in Asia are reflected in their discussions.

S. Hun Kim & Wonsuk Ma (eds.)
Korean Diaspora and Christian Mission
2011-978-1-870345-91-0 / 301pp

As a 'divine conspiracy' for Missio Dei, the global phenomenon of people on the move has shown itself to be invaluable. In 2004 two significant documents concerning Diaspora were introduced, one by the Filipino International Network and the other by the Lausanne Committee for World Evangelization. These have created awareness of the importance of people on the move for Christian mission. Since then, Korean Diaspora has conducted similar research among Korean missions, resulting in this book

Jin Huat Tan
Planting an Indigenous Church
The Case of the Borneo Evangelical Mission
2011 / 978-1-870345-99-6 / 343pp

Dr Jin Huat Tan has written a pioneering study of the origins and development of Malaysia's most significant indigenous church. This is an amazing story of revival, renewal and transformation of the entire region chronicling the powerful effect of it evident to date! What can we learn from this extensive and careful study of the Borneo Revival, so the global Christianity will become ever more dynamic.

Bill Prevette

Child, Church and Compassion

Towards Child Theology in Romania

2012 / 978-1-908355-03-4 / 377pp

Bill Prevett comments that "children are like 'canaries in a mine shaft'; they provide a focal point for discovery and encounter of perilous aspects of our world that are often ignored." True, but miners also carried a lamp to see into the subterranean darkness. This book is such a lamp. It lights up the subterranean world of children and youth in danger of exploitation, and as it does so travels deep into their lives and also into the activities of those who seek to help them.

Samuel Cyuma

Picking up the Pieces

The Church and Conflict Resolution in South Africa and Rwanda

2012 / 978-1-908355-02-7 / 411pp

In the last ten years of the 20th century, the world was twice confronted with unbelievable news from Africa. First, there was the end of Apartheid in South Africa, without bloodshed, due to responsible political and Church leaders. The second was the mass killings in Rwanda, which soon escalated into real genocide. Political and Church leaders had been unable to prevents this crime against humanity. In this book, the question is raised: can we compare the situation in South Africa with that in Rwanda? Can Rwandan leaders draw lessons from the peace process in South Africa?

GENERAL REGNUM TITLES

Vinay Samuel, Chris Sugden (eds.)
The Church in Response to Human Need
1987 / 1870345045 / xii+268pp

Philip Sampson, Vinay Samuel, Chris Sugden (eds.)
Faith and Modernity
Essays in modernity and post-modernity
1994 / 1870345177 / 352pp

Klaus Fiedler
The Story of Faith Missions
1994 / 0745926878 / 428pp

Douglas Peterson
Not by Might nor by Power
A Pentecostal Theology of Social Concern in Latin America
1996 / 1870345207 / xvi+260pp

David Gitari
In Season and Out of Season
Sermons to a Nation
1996 / 1870345118 / 155pp

David. W. Virtue
A Vision of Hope
The Story of Samuel Habib
1996 / 1870345169 / xiv+137pp

Everett A Wilson
Strategy of the Spirit
J.Philip Hogan and the Growth of the Assemblies of God Worldwide, 1960 - 1990
1997 /1870345231/214

Murray Dempster, Byron Klaus, Douglas Petersen (Eds)
The Globalization of Pentecostalism
A Religion Made to Travel
1999 / 1870345290 / xvii+406pp

Peter Johnson, Chris Sugden (eds.)
Markets, Fair Trade and the Kingdom of God
Essays to Celebrate Traidcraft's 21st Birthday
2001 / 1870345193 / xii+155pp

Robert Hillman, Coral Chamberlain, Linda Harding
Healing & Wholeness
Reflections on the Healing Ministry
2002 / 978-1- 870345-35- 4 / xvii+283pp

David Bussau, Russell Mask
Christian Microenterprise Development
An Introduction
2003 / 1870345282 / xiii+142pp

David Singh
Sainthood and Revelatory Discourse
An Examination of the Basis for the Authority of Bayan in Mahdawi Islam
2003 / 8172147285 / xxiv+485pp

For the up-to-date listing of the Regnum books see www.ocms.ac.uk/regnum

Regnum Books International

Regnum is an Imprint of The Oxford Centre for Mission Studies
St. Philip and St. James Church
Woodstock Road
Oxford, OX2 6HR
Web: www.ocms.ac.uk/regnum